Don Taylor
1972

Carlyle Bennett
Golden Gate Seminary
Mill Valley

D1273300

The
**CHURCH
STAFF**
and Its
WORK

The
CHURCH
STAFF
and Its
WORK

W. L. HOWSE

BROADMAN PRESS • Nashville, Tennessee

WA20
H 847c

© 1959 · BROADMAN PRESS
Nashville, Tennessee

All rights reserved
International copyright secured

422–07176

Library of Congress catalog card number: 59–5857

Printed in the United States of America

5. S 58 K.S.P.

To:

The Broadway, Polytechnic, and University Baptist churches, Fort Worth, Texas; Seventh and James Baptist Church, Waco, Texas; and the First Baptist Church, Dallas, Texas, on whose staffs the author was privileged to serve.

Foreword _____

A book on the church staff has been needed for a long time. In recent years many church staff positions have come into being without the benefit of literature to guide the people entering these vocations or the churches they have served. Progress in defining and stabilizing these vocations has been slow and difficult, accompanied by much trial and error.

Thus, many problems have confronted anyone who attempted to write a book in this field. Who could speak for the hundreds of churches which have developed staff programs and enlisted personnel to occupy staff positions? Is it possible to reach agreement on duties and responsibilities of staff members which will apply to the needs of churches in a convention which is now practically nationwide in its ministry? "Who then is equal to these things?"

Of course, the answer is that "No one is equal to these things." Whereas the book has one author, it has many contributors, most of whom cannot be named. Hundreds of such contributors are former students who discussed these matters in classes on the work of the church staff. Many other contributions were made in workshops, conferences, and assemblies. Other ideas came in conferences with pastors and church committees seeking staff personnel. Some contributions were made in conferences with staff members who faced various personal and professional problems.

In addition, seminary professors and the professional staff of the Baptist Sunday School Board have made invaluable suggestions which have been incorporated in the manuscript.

Thus, the ideas advanced in the manuscript are neither official nor are they one man's opinion. Instead, they represent a composite of thought regarding one of the most vital areas of Southern Baptist life. What is written cannot be considered as final. The field of religious education is expanding so rapidly the manuscript will need some revision before it is published. Such need should occasion genuine pleasure since it is an indication of the advancement being made in this field.

It is the hope of the author that from his setting forth the significant responsibilities of staff members in book form the vocations will be stabilized and more effective work and more harmonious interpersonal relationships will result.

Contents _____

The Educational Ministry
of the Pastor

A church in reality should be a school in Christian living. The activities of church members, whether right or wrong, have educational aspects because these activities are highly influential. The planned educational program cannot rise above the general life of the congregation. If the church is to do its work acceptably, not only must it have adequate planned educational processes but all phases of church life must be conducted in terms of Christian ideals. All of the church program must be considered.

Since congregational life is educative, the pastor is immediately concerned with the processes of learning. How can he lead the members of his church to conduct a school in Christian living?

In addition to his preaching and pastoral work, the educational ministries of a church offer a pastor the best possible means for accomplishing such an objective. Every pastor can be effective as preacher and educator. If his concept of the ministry involves both preaching and teaching, a pastor can utilize the organizations of his church to fulfil his ministry to people. The four organizations in Southern Baptist churches are the Sunday school (which includes the Vacation Bible school), the Training Union, the Woman's Missionary Union, and the Brotherhood. These organizations for teaching and training are the hands and feet of a church. If its work is done well, the church must give full support to its preaching and educational ministries.

Although the Music Ministry, because of its service responsibilities to the educational organizations and to the church, is seldom considered as a church educational organization, it does have educational functions. The graded choir program provides basic learning opportunities for its members. The congregation learns much of its theology and many other truths from music. The hymnal, a storehouse of spiritual knowledge, becomes a textbook under proper leadership; thus in this chapter and subsequent ones references to the educational organizations will include the educational aspects of the Music Ministry.

The pastor of a smaller church will have the major responsibility for making the program of teaching and training effective. If he is the only vocational worker in the church, the pastor usually must take the initiative in developing such a program. He will be fortunate if he has a trained group of volunteer leaders to work with him from the beginning of such an endeavor. In most instances he must take the initiative in enlisting and training these workers.

As a rule, the pastor of the medium-sized or large church will have one or more staff members to assist him in his ministry. If these staff members are to render maximum service, the pastor must understand the work of each and be able to counsel with them effectively.

A pastor is more effective in the church education field if he understands the origin and development of the church functions of teaching and training.

I. BIBLICAL BACKGROUNDS

There are many who think that the present-day church education program is of comparatively recent origin. Certain methods and techniques are new; but fundamentally the objectives, content, and functions of this program are not. The teaching ministries of a church are strongly based upon scriptural commands and examples.

1. *The Old Testament*

The Old Testament abounds in commands to teach and in illustrations of the values derived from adequate instruction. Under Old Testament law parents were given the responsibility of guiding the spiritual growth of their children. Thus the home was the primary institution for providing religious teaching for Jewish children.

And these words, which I command thee this day, shall be in thine heart: and thou shalt teach them diligently unto thy children, and shalt talk of them when thou sittest in thine house, and when thou walkest by the way, and when thou liest down, and when thou risest up. And thou shalt bind them for a sign upon thine hand, and they shall be as frontlets between thine eyes. And thou shalt write them upon the posts of thy house, and on thy gates (Deut. 6:6–9).

There was educational significance in the various feasts which were observed in the home. The children went to the Temple on the sabbath day and received instruction through the symbolism and significance of various phases of worship.

Domestic instruction and discipline were ably reinforced by teachers. The priests provided instruction as well as led in the ministrations of worship.

And Moses wrote this law, and delivered it unto the priests the sons of Levi, which bare the ark of the covenant of the Lord, and unto all the elders of Israel. And Moses commanded them, saying, At the end of every seven years, in the solemnity of the year of release, in the feast of tabernacles, when all Israel

is come to appear before the Lord thy God in the place which
he shall choose, thou shalt read this law before all Israel in
their hearing. Gather the people together, men, and women, and
children, and thy stranger that is within thy gates, that they
may hear, and that they may learn, and fear the Lord your God,
and observe to do all the words of this law: and that their children, which have not known any thing, may hear, and learn to
fear the Lord your God, as long as ye live in the land whither
ye go over Jordan to possess it (Deut. 31:9–13).

The tribe of Levi was set apart to be the teachers of the
Jewish people. The entire time of the Levites was devoted to
their work. They were supported from the tithe.

The history of Israel reveals that this nation did not use
God's plan. The priests did not fulfil their responsibilities as
teachers; the people failed in their support and interest;
and the rulers did not encourage the program of instruction.

The failure to teach probably brought into existence the
prophetic office to supplement the ministry of the priests.
This office of prophet developed after the sins of the sons of
Eli. The prophets studied the law, made copies of it, and were
teachers and preachers who denounced national, family,
and personal sins. It was necessary to warn a nation continually of its perversity and tendency toward sin. Their
teaching, which was oral, was effective, and from Samuel to
Malachi there was an adequate supply of men for this work.

An old Jewish proverb, "The true guardians of the city are
the teachers," further indicates the emphasis given to religious instruction.

After the Exile the rabbi was the most important person in
the new order. He was honored above all others. The Jewish
boy gave to him a higher place than to his father because of
the rabbi's influence upon his spiritual life. The rabbi was
the learned teacher who knew the law and could teach its

principles. So important was he in the thinking of the people that a tradition developed concerning a dispute in heaven; a rabbi was called into counsel to settle the matter.

2. *The New Testament*

The educational emphasis in the Old Testament is further developed and enlarged upon in the New Testament. Jesus emphasized teaching throughout his ministry. The word "teacher" is used forty-two times in the Gospels. Christ is spoken of as "teaching" forty-seven times. The content of his message is called "teaching" ten times in the Gospels. Lewis J. Sherrill, in *The Rise of Christian Education,* has given an additional interpretation to this emphasis:

But merely counting words still fails to bring out the place which teaching had in the total ministry of Jesus. Whereas preaching and evangelizing were characteristic of the earlier but not of the later ministry of Jesus, the teaching extended almost to the very end, if we judge by the simple criterion of the location of the passages in the text of the Gospels just as they stand. . . .

So wherever one turns in the ministry of Jesus, he will soon see Jesus teaching. The Gospel which he preached was accompanied by teaching. In proportion as the Gospel of Jesus took hold upon men, the inner nature of that Gospel led by necessity to further teaching concerning the Kingdom which he proclaimed. Without teaching, his Gospel in every probability would have been so grossly misunderstood as to defeat his mission altogether.*

The disciples of Christ also were teachers. The word "disciple" means "learner." These early followers were enrolled in the school of the Master Teacher. After their training they

---

* Lewis J. Sherrill, *The Rise of Christian Education.* (New York: The Macmillan Company, 1944), pp. 87, 89. Used by permission.

were commissioned to teach. It would be impossible to consider their work without the teaching element since they were associated so closely with one who "taught them as one having authority, and not as the scribes" (Matt. 7:29).

Paul also was a teacher. He called himself a teacher as well as an apostle. His ministry abounded in teaching situations. He taught frequently in the synagogues, by the riverside, and in market places, homes, and prisons. He taught representatives of all races who came under his influence. He taught friend, stranger, and enemy. He delivered public discourses, but he was also highly influential in his private teachings (Acts 17:1–3). In his writings Paul told Timothy that one of the qualifications of a minister was that he should be "apt to teach" (1 Tim. 3:2).

Not only did Paul set the pattern in teaching, but in the fields of administration and supervision he gave procedures which are as useful today as they were when first given. He likewise gave instruction regarding church music (Col. 3:16).

Paul maintained contact with the churches which he established and also kept in touch with the new converts. He sought to strengthen, develop, and improve the churches and their members by making return visits as often as possible.

He enlisted others to assist him and trained them for their tasks. One cannot think of Paul without remembering the men who were associated with him. He was responsible for the enlistment of Timothy (Acts 16:1–2). He found Titus and used him in Christian work (Titus 1:5). Some time after an unpleasant experience with John Mark he wrote, "Take Mark, and bring him with thee: for he is profitable to me for the ministry" (2 Tim. 4:11). He mentioned Epaphroditus as "my brother, and companion in labour, and fellowsoldier"

(Phil. 2:25). He encouraged discouraged workers, settled disputes and difficulties, and inspired his associates. He also sought to increase the effectiveness of his ministry by writing letters. He sent messengers to bear these letters and to take his counsel and advice in oral form.

Paul stands out as the master organizer and administrator of the Christian era. One wonders what he would have done were he living today with access to television, radio, telephone, dictating machines, typewriters, and airplanes.

Paul made clear the major objectives of his ministry when he wrote, "Warning every man, and teaching every man in all wisdom; that we may present every man perfect in Christ Jesus" (Col. 1:28).

II. Values of the Educational Ministries

The pastor's place in the educational ministries of a church is based upon the emphases of both the Old and New Testaments. The importance of his position rests also in the carefully analyzed facts of Christian history since the New Testament era. If the work of the churches and the kingdom is to succeed, the pastor must be not only a preacher but also a teacher. It is generally agreed that he must qualify himself as a preacher, but he should also prepare himself to be the church's principal teacher. Many churches have failed to fulfil their missions because the pastors have regarded their educational ministries as something which they could emphasize or not as they desired.

If the work of the church is to be based upon a permanent foundation, the pastor's educational emphasis is not an optional matter. Without the educational viewpoint his work will not have lasting importance. That is, the pastor's work will fail in reaching its greatest usefulness if the people for whom he is responsible are not trained and taught.

The Bible plan is both to preach and to teach the gospel.

There are several reasons why the pastor should invest his time and energies in the educational ministries of his church.

1. *Places of Responsibility for Church Members*

Every church faces the problem of unenlistment. Even in the churches which are well organized only a comparatively few members are doing the major share of the work. Those who are at work are developing more rapidly than those who are idle or who simply attend the worship services. Members who accept responsibility and use their talents in carrying out their tasks are happy, well adjusted, and useful.

If this is true of a few, it is reasonable to suppose that if more jobs were created and more workers were enlisted, the new workers would have similar opportunities for growth and service. Their efforts would also provide an increase in manpower, the effects of which would be felt throughout the church. When the church has positions to be filled, the pastor will find that these opportunities for service give him a tremendous appeal to use in enlisting new workers.

2. *Enlistment for Teaching and Training*

Securing new workers and assigning definite prospects to them for visitation make possible the reaching of larger numbers of individuals for teaching and training. In other years one frequently heard this statement on Sunday, "If everyone present today will come back next Sunday and bring someone with him, we can have twice as many present next Sunday as we have today."

That proposition is true, but it is impossible for two reasons: Not every person present will be back next Sunday, and even if every person present did come back next Sunday, he would not bring someone with him. If each one were given the name and address of a prospect and asked to bring him the next Sunday, such an assignment would be definite enough to get results. But a general appeal will never prove satisfactory.

When a church organizes to reach people and fixes upon its leadership responsibility for doing so, it guarantees that larger numbers of people will be visited, reached, and developed. When, for example, a director accepts the responsibility of a Beginner department in Training Union, her task is to enlist the children in the community who are four and five years of age. Prospects of these ages are assigned to her for visitation and enlistment. Of course, in her visitation this director will seek to enlist every member of the family in Training Union work. What she does for Beginner children and their families would in a graded Training Union be done for persons of all ages. When responsibility is assigned for people of all ages, no person in the community can say truthfully, "No man cared for my soul" (Psalm 142:4). Thus the educational ministry of the church affords the pastor the opportunity of reaching greater numbers of people with the gospel.

3. *Greater Evangelistic Opportunities*

The fully graded Sunday school has been called "the church of tomorrow." This is true because such a large percentage of future church members are now members of the Sunday school. Other organizations of the church make their contributions to evangelism through the training they offer in personal witnessing.

Prospects for membership in the educational organizations are located by a religious census and by checking the church roll to discover those who are not members. These prospects are assigned to the proper workers for visitation. As the members are enrolled, they join in regular Bible study, church membership training, and the Music Ministry under the leadership of consecrated workers. The way of salvation is explained, and problems which hinder acceptance of Christ are solved. Each Sunday, attendance at the worship services is stressed, thereby giving to non-Christians contact with the pastor and members of the church. This fact assures the pastor of an audience in which there are unsaved people. Evangelistic opportunities enlarge under such a program.

4. *Spiritual Growth for Church Members*

After a person accepts Christ and unites with the church, his Christian growth should be guided by the same skilful leadership which led him to Christ. He should be encouraged to pray daily; to read and study his Bible regularly; to take advantage of opportunities for participation, expression, and service in the organizations; and to use his energies, his talents, and his material resources in the service of Christ.

The activities in which each member engages are planned on the basis of his needs at each stage of his development. Under a graded program of teaching and training, the needs of each person may be met at the proper time. This attention to individual needs will assure guidance for each member of the church.

A Junior girl came forward at the close of the morning worship service of her church, making public her profession of faith in Christ. After asking her a few well-phrased questions, the pastor, satisfied that her conversion was genuine, asked the church to vote upon her as a candidate for baptism. When the unanimous vote was taken, the pastor then said, "Now, those of you who also accept the responsibility for this young Christian's growth and maturity and will surround her with the love, sympathy, and guidance needed to grow properly in the Christian faith will say 'Aye.'"

When questioned later about this somewhat unusual vote, the pastor said, "I always ask for such a vote; and sometimes in church business meetings when words become harsh and unkind, I remind our members of their pledge of helpfulness and of the fact that unchristian attitudes hinder the growth of immature Christians."

III. The Pastor's Part

If the educational ministries of his church are to be effective, the pastor must do more than pay lip service to this phase of his ministry.

1. *The Pastor's Heritage*

The educational ministries are stressed in the Old Testament. Jesus emphasized them in his ministry. He commissioned his disciples to evangelize, to baptize, and to continue to teach those who had accepted him. He has promised his presence to those who are faithful in doing these things. The pastor today has the privilege of fulfilling the commission of Christ through attention to the educational phases of his ministry.

2. *Educational Values of the Pulpit Ministry*

The distinctions between preaching and teaching are very slight. A good teacher will do some preaching. A good preacher will do some teaching. An expository sermon planned and delivered so that it is interesting, within the comprehension of the hearers, and directed toward meeting their needs has genuine teaching values.

A pastor does not have to be in a classroom in order to

be a teacher. Each time he preaches, his audience is a potential class. The learning which results from each worship service becomes a part of the total knowledge of the members. The pastor must not become a teacher only, for then his messages would lack the appeal so necessary in effective preaching. But preaching based upon Bible truth will continually teach and develop all who hear it. Pastors who follow such a program of preaching will teach and train their people well.

If the pastor plans all the worship services of the church in such a way that the members are led to have fellowship with God through the leadership of the Holy Spirit, the worshipers will know more of God through this experience than they can know through other channels. Concepts will develop through worship which cannot be as accurately conveyed in any other way.

Nothing aids the church educational program as much as the pulpit ministry of the pastor. Included in his doctrinal preaching should be sermons on the doctrine of Christian growth. Church members must learn that every Christian is born to grow—that spiritual birth implies the need for spiritual growth. Sermons by the pastor will awaken church members to this need.

The place of preaching to bring conviction of sin and repentance in the heart of the sinner is well understood. But preaching is needed also to make clear to the new convert that he is under obligation to accept every possible opportunity for learning, growth, and service offered by his church. In doing so he will have greater assurance of reaching his full stature as a Christian. Many churches have as members numbers of spiritual babies who have not grown since their spiritual birth. These immature Christians must be shown that it is their responsibility to grow and mature. They should be urged to accept every opportunity to exercise their spiritual gifts.

Sermons also are needed which emphasize the importance of the church's providing the best possible learning opportunities for its members. The educational ministries of the church will take on added significance if the pastor preaches frequently on the importance of the church's providing adequate teaching and training opportunities for its constituency. If a church realizes the spiritual significance of its educational functions, then such essential phases of the educational program as enlisting and keeping workers, providing space, equipment, and materials, and enrolling the total constituency will be more rapidly realized.

It is not enough for a church to have the basic educational organizations. Church leaders must know the scriptural reasons for having these organizations and their spiritual significance.

In the two areas just indicated, namely, the necessity for Christian growth and the importance of the church's providing opportunities for this growth, lie untapped preaching opportunities for the pastor. For some reason these areas have been overlooked as sermon subjects. Systematic expository preaching is needed in these fields to awaken individual Christians to their need for growth and to stimulate the church to provide these opportunities for growth.

3. *The Pastor's Understanding of Educational Processes*

Educational processes are slow and tedious. There is drudgery related to learning. There are lessons to be studied, classes to be met, and schedules to be observed.

It is one thing to double the membership of a Sunday school in six months. It is quite another thing to work patiently for six years to educate the same people.

Teaching and training in the church are not spectacular in achievement and seldom produce immediate results. The pastor must not be sidetracked into seeking quick results by superficial methods. The old-fashioned "red and blue" contest will spiral the attendance figures temporarily. But what is its educational value? Time is needed to develop character and stability in Christian living. Realizing this fact and co-operating with the divinely ordained processes for achieving personal growth will assure a quality of personal maturity not possible otherwise.

4. *The Pastor's Preparation for Leadership*

The programs of education and music are developing so rapidly that it is difficult for anyone to keep up with the progress which is being made. To be fully informed regarding these areas of work one must have a knowledge of objectives, content, and methods. Every leader must also understand people and the basic principles of leading them.

To be successful the pastor must have more than a superficial knowledge of religious education and music. He cannot challenge the church's membership in these fields unless he has greater knowledge of the work than the members have. Colleges and seminaries afford each prospective pastor an opportunity to study and understand these phases of his work.

It is interesting that many pastors wish, a year or so after their seminary graduation, that they had taken more courses in religious education and church music. Often they have found themselves trying to lead volunteer workers who are better informed in churchmanship than they. And even where this situation does not exist, these graduates have realized too late that they failed to avail themselves of studies which would have made their ministry far more effective.

This emphasis on training does not mean that complete technical training is required. Certainly the pastor does not have to be trained to direct music, although such skills would be extremely valuable for him. Rather, his training should develop appreciation of religious education and music as ministries of the church and lead him to strengthen the contributions of these ministries in the churches where he serves. For those who cannot attend colleges and seminaries, extension courses offer valuable aid in preparing for church leadership.

The regular training course and study course books are further sources of information for the pastor as he leads the educational organizations in their work. The pastor must study books in these areas at every opportunity, but ultimately he must know the work through actual experience with it. He will find that, as a combination, study and experience have no equal. As he proceeds in his work, he will learn that people in certain situations respond differently; thus methods must be adjusted to local needs without sacrificing basic principles.

5. *The Pastor's Support*

If heavy responsibilities in other areas of his ministry do not permit a pastor to give a sufficient amount of time to religious education and church music, he should lead the church to employ one or more staff members for this work. If such employment is not possible, the pastor must rely upon volunteer workers until staff leadership may be secured. Later, when a church has employed capable people, the pastor should give a suitable portion of his time to helping these staff members plan and promote the work.

In giving emphasis to the educational ministries, the pastor will not subordinate his pastoral and preaching ministries to them. Rather, he will enhance his pastoral and preaching ministries through an adequate program of teaching and training in his church.

Even though the volunteer leaders are well prepared in education and music, the pastor should give emphasis to these fields both publicly and privately. In the worship services he has the opportunity of influencing the largest number of people. In these services he can create sentiment for the educational ministries of his church that will greatly accelerate what is being done through them. In all of his personal contacts he can create sustaining sentiment for this work.

6. *The Pastor's Assistance in Planning*

Any program responsible for reaching, teaching, winning, training, and developing people should not be left to chance. The lives and souls of individuals, the growth and service of the church, and the success of the pastor's ministry are involved in the functions of the church organizations. Surely it is not a question of whether or not the pastor can afford to give his time to this phase of his ministry. The time which he spends in planning the total educational work of the church with those in leadership positions will pay the greatest possible dividends.

The various opportunities open to the pastor for offering guidance in planning the program for the educational ministries will be discussed later.

7. *The Pastor Communicating His Vision*

A pastor's work will have lasting value if he succeeds in gathering about him a group of people who will not only catch his vision but will also share his enthusiasm for the various enterprises of the church. The ministry of the pastor can never be completely successful until it receives proper support from a faithful and dependable group of leaders in the church.

A pastor will find that communicating his vision of the church's future is a slow process and lacks much of the enthusiasm connected with other phases of pastoral work. Yet this is the sure way to develop the necessary leaders and grow a stable and successful church. Only as the volunteer workers begin to dream of the future with their pastor will progress and stability result.

A seminary student was called to the pastorate of a church in a small rural community. This church had been pastored by a succession of students, most of whom had come to the community on week ends, assumed most of the responsibilities for church leadership themselves, and left the members of the church largely to their own resources in their development as leaders.

This new pastor, however, took a different approach. He prepared and delivered sermons to the best of his ability, but he did more. He began to visit in the homes of the members. From these visits he learned the history of the church, the good and the bad in interpersonal relationships, and the abilities and aspirations of his members. After a period of study and evaluation he established a church council and with the heads of the church organizations outlined a year's educational program for the church.

As a result of this program a religious census was taken, the organizations were enlarged, new workers were enlisted and trained, a weekly officers and teachers' meeting and a monthly officers' council were established, and regular visitation was begun. Soon the pastor was preaching to the largest congregations in the history of the church. People were won to Christ, enlisted in study and training, and given responsibilities in the church organizations. The church budget increased, and the church led the association in per capita gifts to missions.

This seminary student knew how to utilize the educational ministries of his church in performing his responsibilities as pastor. Because of the progress of the church he remained its pastor until he completed his graduate degree at the seminary. He now serves a larger church where, with a staff, he continues the same type of effective ministry.

2

The Church Staff
Becomes Necessary

"And God hath set some in the church, first apostles, secondarily prophets, thirdly teachers . . ." (1 Cor. 12:28).

Members of New Testament churches had diverse gifts which were used by the Holy Spirit. As the present-day church staff program develops, the Holy Spirit continues to use the various talents and abilities of his followers even as he did in New Testament times. Through the expansion of this pattern, the churches seem to be returning to the New Testament concept of a functioning church. Several factors have contributed to using the various talents of staff members.

I. REASONS FOR THE GROWTH OF THE CHURCH STAFF

The church staff program has developed in answer to many needs which have been felt acutely by the churches. This development was not planned deliberately. It grew as churches sought to solve the increasing demands made upon them. Various factors have influenced the growth of the church staff pattern.

1. *The Task of Reaching the Multitudes*

In spite of the progress being made, the task of reaching the multitudes is a staggering one. Further, it is difficult to

19

enrol church members in Bible study and membership training. Perhaps one third of the resident church members are not enrolled in Sunday school. The percentage of church members enrolled in the other church organizations is even smaller. It is estimated that 20 per cent of the church members give 80 per cent of the amount contributed through church budgets. Ordinarily the ratio of church members to baptisms is twenty or twenty-three to one.

The task of enrolling for study and training those who are unreached is greater than the task of enrolling the church members. It is estimated that there are in this country thirty-five to forty million unchurched youth under twenty-one years of age. Slightly less than 38 per cent of the total population has no religious affiliation. A larger percentage of these individuals will be enrolled in regular Bible study and training when skilled vocational personnel guide the volunteer workers in reaching them.

2. *The Demand for a Higher Quality of Work*

The program of training volunteer workers in the churches has been underway for many years. Due to this training, the standard of achievement in the churches has been raised so that volunteer workers are now seeking trained vocational personnel to lead them in developing the educational ministries of their churches along better lines. They desire and need skilled vocational workers to give them guidance and supervision.

The advances made by public schools have also contributed to this demand. The erection of new public school buildings and the provision of adequate equipment and improved methods of teaching have often created embarrassing contrasts with the space, equipment, and methods of a church's educational program. The progress of public school music has focused attention upon the need for an adequate church music program. Perhaps the contrast was at first more noticeable to the children and youth than it appeared to workers in the churches. But this contrast between public education and religious education is becoming increasingly obvious to church workers, and they are seeking to close the gap.

3. *The Need for Volunteer Workers*

Another reason why vocational workers are needed is that volunteer workers must be enlisted and trained. In smaller churches the pastor carries the major share of this responsibility. But as the church grows, the need for workers outgrows the pastor's ability to meet the demand.

Perhaps the most pressing problem in every church is the need for more and better volunteer workers. It is safe to assume that a sufficient number of prospective workers may be found in every church to take care of the work to be done. If these workers cannot be found in the membership of the church, they live in the community; they must be reached, won, and enlisted in church membership before being elected to positions of leadership.

The leadership problem is acute, partly because there is such a rapid change in the personnel of most church organizations. In larger churches resignations occur each week. At certain seasons of the year there may be as many as thirty or forty vacant positions of leadership in a church. The problem, on a proportionate basis, is just as great in the smaller churches.

The training of these volunteer workers is another phase of this same problem. Most workers are untrained and unprepared for leadership work when they are enlisted. The promise of training is often a great incentive to those who desire to serve but feel inadequate for their tasks.

Developing an adequate training program is also a responsibility calling for skill and time on the part of someone in the church. Periods of study must be planned. Teachers must be enlisted, and suitable textbooks must be chosen. Records of awards must be kept. Recognition of the work must be made through banquets, commencement exercises, or other means.

By careful advance planning and enlistment many of the churches now are recruiting prospective workers before they are needed. Some churches give these workers formal training in advance of their assignments. This advance textbook training is supplemented by practice teaching and observation so that the prospective workers may have some experience before they assume their positions. Many churches, through advance planning, have a waiting list of qualified workers and have reduced to a minimum the number of resignations caused by discouragement.

4. *The Growth of the Educational Organizations*

The churches which are succeeding with their educational ministries make large use of their organizations for teaching and training. These churches elect the workers, guide the program of instruction and activities, and emphasize the work of these organizations in their programs. Some individuals who are skeptical of using these organizations look upon them as being mechanical. Sometimes it has been true that the chief end of a leader's work has been an organization itself rather than the use of the organization in developing individuals and growing a church. It should be remembered, however, that church organizations are composed of people, and people are never mechanical.

Although organizations are not mechanical, there are specific techniques which apply to each organization. These techniques must be understood and applied if the organization is to function at its best. For example, basic to the life of each educational organization is its numerical growth. There are special techniques for keeping an organization healthy enough to grow in membership.

Each organization must provide for every person who should be enrolled. When maximum growth has been reached, the organization must be enlarged so that its work of enlistment may continue. Knowing when and how to enlarge the organization demands much study and time on the part of someone in the church. Churches are realizing that vocational workers with special training, skills, and experience are needed to diagnose the needs of the organizations and lead in a continuous program of enlargement and enlistment.

5. *The Correlation of the Work*

The need for correlation is another factor which has increased the demand for a church staff. Each of the educational organizations has certain basic functions to perform. Each organization came into being to meet needs not being met by existing organizations. Such origin indicates that each organization has a vital role to fill in the educational program of the church. Yet each cannot operate independently within a church, for common demands will be made upon the same constituency by all organizations.

The Music Ministry functions in part through its graded choir program. But music is also a part of every phase of a church's program. Thus it is important for the educational aspects of the Music Ministry to be correlated with the other educational work of the church.

Some staff member or group of staff members is needed to correlate the work of these organizations so that each member of the church may secure the maximum contributions which these organizations can provide. This correlation calls for a person or persons who by training and experience can give proper emphasis to each organization and fit it into its proper place of service in the church.

6. *The Trend Toward Specialization*

Specialization within various age groups has been a decided trend in the educational ministries during recent years. Lesson courses, textbooks, music and other materials, methods, procedures, space, and equipment reflect this trend. As specialization has taken place, organizations have enlarged until one staff member cannot give the guidance needed by the various volunteer workers.

Sunday schools in some churches have two Cradle Roll, ten Nursery, four Beginner, six Primary, eight Junior, eight Intermediate, four Young People's, and eight Adult departments. The Training Unions have a corresponding number of departments. Woman's Missionary Unions have multiple Sunbeam Bands, Girls' Auxiliaries, and Young Woman's Auxiliaries, and the Brotherhoods have multiple Royal Ambassador chapters. Many churches now have numbers of song leaders and pianists, numerous choirs, and hundreds of choir members. Adults who serve as workers in such churches number several hundred.

In these churches directors of children's, youth, and adult work are needed to master the specialized materials and methods for these age groups in the church organizations. Some churches provide only one vocational worker for the entire children's division, but a few of the larger churches are employing a staff member for each of the various age divisions, such as Cradle Roll, Nursery, Beginner, Primary, and Junior. The same churches employ a director of Intermediate work and a director of Young People's work. These persons do not direct music for their age groups unless they are specifically trained in music. A few churches are now employing directors of adult work.

7. *The Demands of Growing Churches*

Growing churches require adequate vocational personnel. As a church grows in membership, the pastor will face increasing difficulty in giving adequate time and attention to each phase of church life. The church must realize the problems created by this situation and secure the necessary staff members to share these growing responsibilities with the pastor. When these workers are added to the staff, the pastor does not hold or relinquish all responsibilities in the educational field. Instead, the church expects him to share these responsibilities with staff members who are dedicated to specialized phases of the church's ministry. This division of labor will enable the pastor to devote himself more to his preaching and pastoral ministries and, at the same time, make sure that the church's constituency is reached, taught, won, and trained adequately.

A church with three hundred to four hundred members needs a full-time staff member in addition to the pastor. If the church does not have an additional staff member by the time the church membership reaches five hundred, not only the pastor but also many members of the church will have recognized the pressing needs for such a worker. As the membership of the church increases, a new staff member will be needed for each five to six hundred members.

8. *The Importance of the Educational Organizations*

It has been estimated that 85 to 95 per cent of the church members, 85 per cent of the church workers, and 95 per cent of those now serving in church-related vocations have come from the educational program. Music also is a means of enlistment. Churches with a complete Music Ministry are reaching, winning, and enlisting large numbers of individuals. These outstanding results have been accomplished in spite of the fact that many churches have not taken their educational functions seriously.

The provision of educational facilities, the demand for a higher quality of work, the improvement of methods and procedures, and many other factors have created an unprecedented demand for a trained vocational leadership in the churches.

II. Procedure for Calling Staff Members

Extending a call to a staff member involves more than employment. Basically it involves an earnest effort to follow divine leadership in finding the right person for each staff position. A church should pray earnestly before seeking to locate the proper person for each leadership responsibility. In this way the church will not make the mistake of simply asking God to bless its efforts in finding someone. Instead, the church can ask to be led to the person who can serve it best. Also, prayer will keep the church from simply "hiring" a staff member when it should be seeking to find God's will in choosing a leader for a divinely appointed task. There are basic principles to follow if staff members are to be enlisted properly.

1. *Beginning with the Need*

This beginning point seems obvious, but it is frequently overlooked. One church is likely to follow the example of another. For example, if one church has a minister of education, another church may feel it needs a similar worker. However, an analysis of the needs of this same church may reveal that a minister of education and music is needed. If a church cannot establish the need for a worker, it will be difficult for him to be fully accepted by the membership of the church.

2. Informing the Church

If a staff member is needed, the next step is to inform the church. This may be done in several ways. The pastor might mention the need to the entire congregation, giving basic information regarding contemplated responsibilities. If the church has a personnel committee, this committee should write a position description indicating the major tasks of such a staff position.

It is unfair to the prospective staff member to approach him about a position in the church until the church knows that the need for such a position exists and authorizes the new office to be created.

Knowing the need will assist the church in reaching a conviction regarding the value of such a position to the church. This conviction will also help in making the new staff member feel he is needed and wanted, in making provision for his coming, and in working with him after he arrives on the field.

3. Appointing a Committee *

Although the church usually gives the pastor the privilege of locating a new staff member, it will be far better if the personnel committee works closely with the pastor in securing such a worker. It is a mistake at any time to elect a worker without the support of the church membership. The new

---

* See also the *Church Committee Manual* (Nashville: Convention Press, 1958).

staff member must serve not only with the pastor but with the church members. If they are lukewarm toward him and his responsibilities, he may never win their support.

The personnel committee should be composed of individuals who know the needs of the church and who can present these needs forcefully to prospective workers.

4. Securing Recommendations

Since there is such a demand for staff members, good prospects are difficult to locate.

One fruitful source is the list of graduates of Southern Baptist seminaries. All of these seminaries now have schools or departments of religious education and church music which train scores of students every year for this type of service. Professors in these seminaries are able to provide information regarding their graduates and are always glad to co-operate in making this information available to the churches. If it is possible to visit one of these institutions, a committee may interview prospective staff members there, as well as secure information concerning them from the proper sources.

State secretaries of Sunday School, Training Union, Brotherhood, Woman's Missionary Union, Church Music, and Baptist Student Union departments often are able to give information concerning prospective workers. Leaders in Southern Baptist Convention agencies have wide contacts and are able to be of service in this matter.

Pastors with whom workers have served may indicate the quality of their service. Staff members in the churches may know of fellow workers in other churches who may be available.

There are state and regional organizations of staff members. Information may be secured from the presidents and

by attending regular meetings of these organizations. With
so many opportunities for information available it is unfortunate if pastors and committee members overlook the importance of thorough investigation.

5. *Arranging a Personal Interview*

Much of the success of enlistment depends upon initial
contacts. Conviction regarding the need for this staff member and his fitness for the task will give assurance to the pastor and the committee. The prospect will be impressed with
a joint approach by the pastor and the committee. This action will assure him that both the pastor and the church are
united in their efforts toward his enlistment. Meeting face to
face will afford the opportunity for discussion. This method
is worth dozens of letters and telephone calls.

In the initial interview and in succeeding contacts the
pastor and committee should make it clear that finding God's
will in the matter is the most important consideration for all
concerned.

6. *Presenting Duties of Office*

During the first interview many important matters should
be discussed. The committee should point out why a staff
member is needed. Problems which he will face in accomplishing his task should be presented. Duties of the office
should be discussed. During this part of the interview, the
pastor and committee should indicate what they will expect
of the worker and ask for his impressions and reactions to
what they have said. In the free give and take of such discussions, definite opinions will be formed.

The committee also should indicate the amount of time
the church is willing for the staff member to devote to outside meetings, such as revivals, enlargement campaigns, con-

ventions, and assemblies. They should specify the length of
vacation periods.

The questions of salary, housing, car expenses, and retire-
ment should be included as a part of the entire presentation.
Whether or not the church will take care of the expense of
moving a staff member should also be considered. Often busi-
nessmen on a committee are inclined to feel that adding a
member to the staff should follow much the same procedure
as hiring an employee in their organizations. Frequently they
put their questions bluntly, "What will you come for?" or
"What will it take to get you?" A person who has been called
of God to serve in a church-related vocation will not appreciate the fact that his Christian service is being evaluated
solely on a monetary basis and will refuse to consider the
offer if the salary is the main appeal.

The prospective worker is entitled to know the financial
consideration along with the other phases of the work, but
he should not be sought purely on the basis of material in-
ducements. He should not be asked to indicate the amount
of salary he thinks he should have. If he is asked for an opinion regarding his salary, the prospective staff member should
indicate that he is leaving this matter with the pastor, the
committee, and the church. The conference should be closed
with prayer that God's leadership may be made clear to each
member of the group.

7. *Arranging for a Visit*

Since they are to work together, it is well for the person
under consideration and the church members to meet one
another before a call is extended. Visiting the church will
give everyone a better understanding of the fitness of the
worker for the task. The expense involved in such a visit will
prove to be a worthwhile investment for the church. If a visit

is made, some time should be spent in group meetings and personal interviews with those with whom the vocational worker is to serve.

8. *Making the Decision a Matter of Prayer*

Prayer should pervade all conferences concerning any church position. Neither the church nor the worker would knowingly make a mistake. However, some excellent leaders have been mistaken about their places of service, and much unhappiness has resulted for both the workers and the churches they sought to serve.

The most important factor in the decision is the will of God for the church and the prospect. The church should be asked to pray that the person under consideration may have the clear leadership of the Lord in reaching the proper decision.

9. *Recommending a Call*

If the committee is confident that the prospect is the person for the place, and if he indicates he will accept the work if called, the committee should recommend that the church extend him a call. Should the recommendation meet with opposition, the worker should be so notified, and the church should weigh the difficulties involved before reaching a definite conclusion as to what should be done. Every worker needs the support of a strong majority, but undue emphasis often is placed upon a unanimous call. Even if the call is unanimous, the spirit of unanimity may change soon after the new staff member arrives.

Of course, if the vote of the church is enthusiastic, the prospective worker may take this as an added indication of the opportunities the new position will afford him for service to the church.

10. *Preparing the Church*

Such preparation is always in order. It is needed especially if the church has never had such a staff member before. Much of his success will depend upon how well his work is understood by all members of the church.

Through public statements, articles in the church paper, conferences with key workers, and private contacts the pastor and the committee can prepare the way for the coming of the new worker. Explaining his duties and responsibilities and the various commitments made by the church will clarify what the new worker is to do. By exercising skill and judgment, the pastor and committee can prepare the way for the coming of the staff member and give him the proper atmosphere and climate in which to begin the work he is to do in the church.

The pastor of a growing church began to feel the need for the assistance of additional staff personnel. Realizing that members of the church would have to realize the need also, he requested the church to appoint a committee to determine if such a need existed. A representative committee was appointed and began its work. Committee members corresponded with churches of comparable size and location. Visits were made to some of these churches and additional data were secured. The committee made a survey of the work of their church and found that only a fraction of their potential was being realized.

As a result of this study the committee recommended the immediate employment of a secretary and the future employment of a minister of education and music. The church enthusiastically adopted the committee's report, and a church staff program was begun on a sound basis.

3

The Minister of Education
and the
Associate Pastor

"Who is a minister of education?" "What is a minister of education supposed to do?" These and similar questions have been raised with increasing frequency by pastors, ministers of education, personnel committees, and other church members during recent years. Even some who are serving as ministers of education want these questions answered.

The duties of the minister of education have lacked clear definition and general agreement. There are many reasons for this lack of clarification, one of which is the diversity of church situations and needs. This position is also a comparatively new vocation, although its basic functions are centuries old.

Another difficult problem involved in a clear definition of responsibilities is the use of different titles to designate the minister of education. Some of the titles used most frequently are educational director, director of religious education, assistant pastor, assistant to the pastor, associate pastor, associate to the pastor, religious work director, director of religious activities, and director of church activities. This use of numerous titles indicates clearly the need for a definition of duties. In many instances, when a minister of education has been employed, the church has not understood clearly what he was to do, and the worker himself has not understood his duties.

In the early days of his vocational service the writer shared in the worship services of his church by recognizing the presence of visitors and interpreting the educational opportunities of the week to church members. During a week following such participation in Sunday's services the writer and his pastor were visiting some of the members together. One of the members was clear as to the duties of the pastor but puzzled over the responsibilities of the minister of education. A brief explanation of these responsibilities seemed to leave her even more confused. Finally, after another attempt at a description the light seemed to dawn, and she exclaimed, "Oh, you make the announcements on Sunday morning!"

I. The Minister of Education

A minister of education is a person called of God, adequately trained, and employed by a church to devote all, or the major portion, of his time to the educational work of the church. The minister of education works with the pastor in making all of the life of the church educational. He also serves with the volunteer workers in the Sunday school, Vacation Bible school, Training Union, Woman's Missionary Union, and Brotherhood, helping them to achieve their objectives and improve the quality of their work. He co-operates with the minister of music and supervises other staff members in the development of their programs.

II. Duties of the Minister of Education

When a pastor is the only vocational worker in a church, the major responsibility for the educational program rests upon him. The election of a minister of education will call for a division of responsibility between the two. The pastor then will share his educational ministry with the minister of education, planning the work with him and using his influence to guarantee the success of this new relationship.

The program of the church is a total program in which every staff member must have a vital interest. The minister of education will seek to advance the total ministry of the church.

1. *Co-operate with the Pastor and Other Staff Members*

Since theirs is a shared ministry, every minister of education must work in full co-operation with his pastor. The failures and successes of these two are wrapped up together. If either fails, his failure will affect the work of the other. They must learn how to differ in a spirit of Christian love and yet work together for the good of the entire church.

The minister of education must look to the pastor for leadership in the entire program of the church. If he works independently of the pastor, he will create grievous problems for himself and ultimately defeat his ministry.

No worker should ever use his position to create problems and leave lasting scars as reminders of his unfortunate ministry. The church employs him to strengthen its work, not to weaken it. Only a friendly, cordial, co-operative attitude will make for successful staff relationships.

2. *Understand the Major Objectives of the Work*

It is necessary for the minister of education to have purpose and direction in his work. If the ultimate objectives of his work are not clear to him, it will be impossible for him to make them clear to others. It is more likely that the minister of education will have the co-operation of others if they understand the aims which they are seeking with and through him and find these aims to be desirable. Only as there is agreement upon objectives can there be high morale and unity of action.

The minister of education's aims should involve what is to be accomplished with, by, and for people. They should also set forth what is to be accomplished for the church. The educational organizations which are necessary in accomplishing these aims are not to become ends in themselves but are the means of reaching the objectives which have been set up by the minister of education.

Recently the Baptist Sunday School Board formulated a statement of objectives to guide its educational and editorial personnel in their work. A study of this statement should prove helpful to staff members who are interested in stating objectives for their work. A condensed statement of the major objectives is as follows:

1. To lead each person to a genuine experience of the forgiving and saving grace of God through Jesus Christ.

2. To guide each person into intelligent, active, and devoted membership in a New Testament church.

3. To help each person to make Christian worship a vital and constant part of his expanding experience.

4. To help each person to know the Bible; the great realities of the Christian faith; the history and status of the Christian movement; and the history, distinctive beliefs, and practices of his own denomination; and to develop deep and abiding Christian convictions concerning all these matters.

5. To assist each person in developing such Christian attitudes and appreciations in every area of experience that he will have a Christian approach to all of life.

6. To guide each person in developing habits and in learning techniques which promote personal spiritual growth, and

in accepting and applying Christian standards of personal and social conduct in every area of life.

7. To guide each person to invest his talents and to develop skills in Christian service.*

+3. *Develop Appreciation of Educational Work*

Developing an appreciation among church members of the values of the ministries of teaching and training is an important responsibility of the minister of education. This responsibility is especially important if he is the first such worker whom a church employs. Church members should be led to recognize the contributions which are made to individuals and the church through an adequate educational ministry. If these members are committed to the importance of the teaching and training ministries of the church, they will be willing to contribute their efforts and financial support to such a program.

The entire church either creates or fails to create the climate in which Christian growth takes place. Parents who send their children to the church instead of attending with them create a negative climate in which the church finds little encouragement and support. The concept of the church itself as an educational institution must be conveyed to all church members.

4. *Recommend Prospective Workers*

The minister of education should have on file a list of competent people to recommend for enlistment to department superintendents, department directors, and the leadership of the Woman's Missionary Union and the Brotherhood. He

* Church staff members may have the complete statement upon request to Clifton J. Allen, Editorial Secretary, 127 Ninth Avenue, North, Nashville 3, Tennessee.

must also be prepared to suggest prospective church committee members, ushers, and church officers. This list should be compiled in conference with the pastor and the heads of the church organizations.

Some churches have a committee to survey leadership possibilities throughout the year. If the church has such a committee, the minister of education will work closely with it. Without this committee the minister of education must take the initiative in preparing a list of potential leaders. To know who they are, he should maintain close contact with as many church members as possible so that he may know how to use their talents and interests to the best advantage. Few weeks will pass without some resignation or change of leadership. Workers must be enlisted immediately after each resignation if an adequate program of work is to be maintained.

Much of the responsibility for the enlistment of workers depends upon the departmental leaders. New workers are loyal to the one who enlists them. The leadership of the department superintendent and department director is strengthened when they play a vital role in enlisting workers for their departments.

5. *Lead in Developing Workers*

Although the minister of education is concerned with the spiritual growth of all church members, he must spend most of his time in developing the volunteer workers in the church. As he trains capable leaders, he will be able to provide the proper spiritual guidance for all church members. Paul gave an emphasis to developing workers when he wrote, "And the things that thou hast heard of me among many witnesses, the same commit thou to faithful men, who shall be able to teach others also" (2 Tim. 2:2).

Here is an opportunity for the minister of education to

function as a teacher, sharing his knowledge and experience with those who have accepted the challenge to prepare for leadership. Perhaps the minister of education is nearer to the center of his vocation as he becomes a teacher of church leaders than at any other time.

6. Counsel Workers and Members

Group and personal counseling will occupy a prominent place in the daily activities of the minister of education. He should be able to assist the volunteer workers in solving problems and improving the quality of their work. These procedures call for special skill and understanding. In addition to his counseling opportunities with church leaders, he should counsel with young people regarding vocations, choice of a university or college, and similar decisions. Often pastors are happy for their staff members to counsel with church members regarding love, courtship, marriage, and family relationships. However, before engaging in such counseling activities, the pastor and minister of education should agree upon whatever division of responsibility is desirable in all these areas.

7. Lead in Securing Suitable Space and Equipment

The minister of education should lead in a program of expansion which will call for enlarged facilities in which to work. If all organizations are to grow, space in which to provide for more units of work must be made available. Growth cannot take place without additional space. It is a difficult task to plan a building so that every phase of work has adequate provision. Such planning calls for the specialized skill and advice which the minister of education should be able to give. Also, securing the best equipment possible has much to do with the effectiveness of the work. Often the usefulness of an expensive building is dissipated by the purchase of the wrong equipment. The minister of education should know the kind of equipment needed and should be given opportunities to recommend it.

Frequently, in providing educational space churches do not make adequate provision for the Training Union. The classrooms of the Junior and Intermediate departments should have movable partitions between alternate classrooms. This will permit the use of these rooms for Junior and Intermediate unions. Otherwise the classrooms will be too small for the unions, and the department assembly rooms will be too large. Attention should be given to providing adequate space for all other age groups. It is especially desirable to provide as much square footage as possible for the Nursery, Beginner, and Primary departments. Since music activities and choirs for Beginners, Primaries, and Juniors are held in their respective departments, adequate space and equipment must be provided.

Provision should also be made for a church library, visual aids, recreation, fellowship, religious dramatics, and the church Music Ministry. These play a vital part in all organizations. The minister of education should know the value of each aid, activity, and ministry and utilize all of them in the educational program.

8. *Serve in Administrative Capacities*

The church will look to the minister of education to get the work done. It is his responsibility to lead in accomplishing the tasks which are determined by the church. For this he is given a certain amount of authority. He should remember that this is given to him in trust and that he is responsible to the church for the way he uses his authority. In all of these tasks he should recognize the pastor's leadership.

The minister of education's ability to understand necessary organizational details and to help leaders apply them will be a great factor in his success. His ability as an executive may be measured by his skill in getting things done with minimum effort and difficulty and by his ability to delegate responsibility to others. He will seek at all times to project the educational program through enlisting and inspiring others. The old saying, "It is better to put ten people to work than it is to do the work of ten people," is particularly applicable here.

9. *Supervise Activities and Personnel*

It is the purpose of supervision to improve all activities and efforts being used in reaching, teaching, winning, and training church members. Supervision will mean the improvement of the total program. It is not enough to organize and set in motion a program of church activities. This program must be studied constantly and analyzed carefully in order to remedy defects, improve the quality of work, and evaluate the results. The minister of education, in conference with the workers in each organization, will endeavor to see that these basic factors are accomplished.

As additional church staff members are elected, the minister of education usually will supervise their work. This supervision will be extended to those involved in the educational phases of the work, such as the educational secretary, the director of children's work, the director of youth work, the director of church recreation, and others.

In some churches the minister of education also supervises all secretaries (except the pastor's secretary), the janitor, and other workers. Care must be taken in enlarging the supervisory activities of the minister of education so as not to weaken his opportunities for maximum service in his major field. When the staff becomes large, a church is wise to employ a church business administrator to take care of the business matters of the church and thus free the minister of education to pursue the work for which he is particularly fitted and trained.

In many churches the minister of education will give assistance in supervising and co-ordinating the work of church committees. These committees can render invaluable service if someone assists them with their work. The minister of education is in a position to render excellent service to them.

If the church has a minister of music, he will have the same relationship with the pastor and church membership as the minister of education. The minister of education will not supervise the minister of music but will work in fullest co-operation with him.

10. *Keep Abreast of Trends in Religious Education*

Keeping up with the progress being made in religious education involves selective buying and reading of books, taking refresher courses, and attending state, regional, and Convention-wide conferences, clinics, and assemblies. If the minister of education succeeds in his work, constant reading and study will be necessary. Methods are constantly changing. Organizational patterns are being revised periodically. If the minister of education is not in touch with these changes, his work will soon become out-of-date.

11. *Be a Personal Soul-Winner*

The minister of education, as a child of God and as a leader of church members, must be a personal soul-winner. He cannot lead the church organizations to be thoroughly evangelistic unless he sets the pace himself. If he leads the organizations to function in personal witnessing, he may know in advance of each Sunday the approximate number of additions to the church which may be expected.

If he succeeds in this task, he must be a student of the Bible and know how to use it in soul-winning. A major weakness of many ministers of education is their lack of knowledge of the Bible. They need to know it for the spiritual strength which it will contribute to their individual lives and for the value it has in bringing lost people to Christ.

III. THE RELATIONSHIPS OF THE MINISTER OF EDUCATION TO THE EDUCATIONAL ORGANIZATIONS

In many churches the minister of education serves as superintendent of the Sunday school and director of the Training Union. In other churches he assists the Sunday school superintendent and the Training Union director in their responsibilities.

The question of which of these two practices is the better procedure is frequently raised. Some churches have used one plan, while some have used the other. Churches which are accustomed to their own plan have much to say in its favor. Ministers of education have their preferences, also. Some prefer to be Sunday school superintendent and Training Union director. Others prefer to work through elected church officers. A choice of plans depends upon the desire of the church and of the minister of education and the effectiveness of the volunteer leadership.

The ministers of education who serve as Sunday school superintendents and Training Union directors feel they can do more effective work if they work directly with the department superintendents of the Sunday school and department directors of the Training Union. They believe, also, that a greater degree of correlation is achieved under such a plan.

Those who favor the other plan feel it is best to leave organizations in the hands of volunteer leadership. In doing so they can train the volunteer workers more adequately for their tasks. They believe that the example of a volunteer general superintendent and general director will produce a greater response on the part of all the other workers.

In meetings of educational workers where this question is discussed the group usually is about evenly divided. However, all agree that in either case the volunteer workers must be trained as adequately as possible. Those who are general superintendents and general directors have as associates volunteer workers who carry much of the responsibility for their organizations.

Regardless of this organizational relationship, the minister of education has basic responsibilities related to the educational organizations of the church.

1. *Utilize the Organizations in Evangelism*

The two main responsibilities of the minister of education are to use the educational organizations of the church in winning lost persons to Christ and in leading those who are won to achieve full Christian maturity. Whatever is necessary to accomplish these important objectives should have the attention and emphasis of the minister of education. The Sunday school (which includes the Vacation Bible school), the Training Union, the Woman's Missionary Union, and the Brotherhood offer the finest opportunities the church has for accomplishing these goals.

2. *Lead the Organizations to Be Church Centered*

There should be no distinction between the objectives of the church and those of the educational organizations. The program for the organizations may be determined by examining the New Testament and discovering there the program of the church. Each organization, properly directed, will never be in conflict with the church. For example, the Sunday school is not separate from the church but is the church engaged in the ministry of teaching. Its officers are elected by the church to give their influence to strengthening the total ministry of the church.

All officers and teachers should attend the worship services of the church regularly. In the truest sense there are not two separate services on Sunday morning—the "Sunday school" and the "church." Both meetings are a unit with special activities and functions fostered by the church. Properly conducted, all that is done on Sunday morning is the work of the church. Workers used to teach children the song, "Sunday school is over, and I am going home. Good-bye! Good-bye!" Such an attitude is misleading. Sunday school is not over until the sermon and invitation have been concluded. This philosophy applies also to the relationship of the Training Union and the Sunday evening service.

3. *Follow a Balanced Educational Program*

The members of the church council have the responsibility of planning and recommending a balanced educational program to the church. The pastor is chairman of the council. Representatives of church organizations and other phases of church educational work are members of the council; they serve with the pastor and minister of education in planning the educational program. The minister of education is expected to have a vital part in advising the educational leadership with reference to planning and conducting this well-balanced program for the year.

Effective work is accomplished when the program is planned well in advance, adopted by the church, and given publicity among the church members.

4. *Assist in Maintaining Adequate Organization*

Each educational agency of the church must have adequate organization if it is to function effectively. It must provide for each age group of its constituency. When each agency reaches the saturation point in enrolment, plans should be made for enlarging its organization so that continuing growth in membership may result. A careful analysis of lists of prospects will reveal the age groups being overlooked by each agency. The groups most frequently overlooked are the men, married and single young people, and babies.

Attention should be given to adhering to the system of grading so that there will be places in the organization for all who should attend. Annual promotion assists in keeping the grading system in operation as nothing else can do.

The organization, once established, must have well qualified workers to make it effective. Vacancies or positions occupied by listless, poorly prepared workers defeat the purpose of the work.

5. *Lead the Organizations in Reaching Their Constituencies*

Too often numerical growth has been the sole measure of the success of the minister of education. Although adding members is within itself an undue emphasis, enrolling members and securing their attendance is the beginning point in meeting the needs of people. People who are irregular in attendance cannot be effectively taught or trained. The minister of education must lead in finding all unreached people and enlisting them in regular attendance, study, and spiritual development.

In seeking to reach all people in the community for regular Bible study and Christian training, the minister of education should emphasize the importance of enrolling parents and working with them in building Christian family life. What the church seeks to do for children and youth is aided greatly by participation and interest of Christian parents.

The minister of education should lead in a continuous effort to win and develop parents, giving them definite instruction in how they may co-operate with the church in the Christian growth of their children. He should help the volunteer workers plan parent-worker meetings designed to develop closer co-operation between home and church. The minister of education should strive for regular visitation in the homes of parents. He should encourage the workers to take and explain the use of materials designed to develop Christian family life.

6. *Guide the Workers in Improvement*

The most serious criticism of present-day religious education is that it is not producing results commensurate with the investments being made in it. Whether this criticism is just or not, the minister of education must be concerned with the quality of work being done.

Time should be given to the workers in the Sunday school, Vacation Bible school, Training Union, Woman's Missionary Union, and Brotherhood to help them in making their work more effective. By meeting with them in their planning meetings, by using available visual aids in instructing them, by emphasizing the study of training course and study course textbooks, and by using various other ways the level of work may be lifted.

7. *Lead the Organizations to Share in Missions*

Woman's Missionary Union majors on missionary education in the church. The minister of education can render genuine service to the program of world missions by co-operating with the leaders in seeking to extend the ministry of this organization to all who should be members of it. He may also assist the leaders of this organization by eliminating conflicts in the church program which interfere with the regular meetings and weeks of prayer of Woman's Missionary Union, by co-operating in their promotion of mission study classes, and by enlisting their help in planning for schools of missions for the church.

The other church organizations have contributions to make to world missions. Regular Bible study undergirds the entire mission enterprise. Training Union, Vacation Bible school, and Brotherhood lesson materials and programs make a distinctive contribution to the world missions program of Southern Baptists.

8. *Develop a Continuous Visitation Program*

No organization will reach its constituency unless its workers are trained to visit regularly and effectively. The minister of education must lead in enlisting and training key leadership who will direct visitation efforts for their respective organizations. Churches having the greatest success with their visitation programs have set a definite day in the week as visitation day. They have developed plans calling for assignments, personal reports, and testimonies.

Training workers in how to visit and having a continued emphasis upon maintaining this ministry throughout the week will eventually produce results.

9. *Seek to Create Denominational Loyalty*

Information concerning denominational activities should be given to the members of all educational organizations as time and occasion permit. The church council will include the emphases in the denominational calendar when it plans the calendar of activities for the church. Programs may then be planned for department assemblies and other meetings in keeping with the emphases of the denomination.

The minister of education should lead all workers to co-operate in the associational meetings of the organizations. The district association is the second unit of Baptist life and is thus a potential agency for developing denominational loyalty. It deserves the full support of every church member.

10. *Inspire the Workers to Develop in Stewardship*

A church grows properly under the right type of leader-ship. Leadership develops as people have a sense of mission and stewardship. Every worker in the church should feel this sense of mission and stewardship in relationship to his tasks. He should have the conviction that God has led him into his work and that the service he renders is his opportunity to witness for Christ. He should have a growing sense of stew-ardship with reference to his time, talents, and money. There is no place for selfishness in such a concept of stewardship.

The minister of education has the privilege of helping all church members develop this sense of stewardship. He may contribute to this concept through the proper enlistment of leaders, interpreting to the workers the significance of their tasks, inspiring them to serve, and pointing them to the ideals revealed in the life of Christ.

In some churches the minister of education is asked to lead the annual church budget subscription program. Since he has close contact with the workers who must carry responsi-bility for this program, he is the logical person to be given this leadership if his other duties will permit. If he does not take the active leadership in this program, he will assist those who do.

11. *Lead in Conducting Effective Meetings*

The minister of education should lead in maintaining an effective Training Union monthly officers' council. This meeting will help co-ordinate the work of all unions and will correlate the various activities. An organization needs some time each month for specific planning. Nothing will take the place of meeting together to make reports and plan the work for the coming month. The minister of education will have an opportunity at this meeting to keep the officers of the Training Union informed regarding their various responsibilities. Use of the Training Union calendar will create a spirit of unity and co-operation among the workers.

The best way to have an efficient Sunday school is to begin with a functioning weekly officers and teachers' meeting. If the minister of education is the superintendent of the Sunday school, he will plan the meeting and preside over it. In addition to presenting plans to the workers, he should provide time for reports from the general officers and give the pastor an opportunity to talk informally to the entire group each week. Having a general meeting of this nature before the departments assemble for their meetings will serve to keep the work of the Sunday school unified. If the minister of education is not the general superintendent, he should assist the superintendent in making plans and securing attendance for the meeting.

The minister of education should so win the confidence and support of the presidents of both the Woman's Missionary Union and the Brotherhood that they will be assured of his interest and seek his help in their programs. He should assist them in scheduling the dates of their business meetings and important committee meetings. The minister of education should supply them with the necessary materials and information to plan their work successfully.

12. *Serve as a Resource Person for All Organizations*

The minister of education must know the duties of the officers and committees of all organizations and be able to counsel with the workers concerning their work. He will also need to know the best methods to be used. He must have a grasp of the division of time for the various elements in the program of each of these organizations. As a student of their work, he should have available in his office the administration books which deal with the methods and techniques of the Sunday school, Vacation Bible school, Training Union, Woman's Missionary Union, and Brotherhood.

If the minister of education is to serve effectively, he must have an accurate knowledge of the history of religious education. He should know when and under what circumstances each of the educational organizations came into being. He should know the basic objectives and functions of each. He needs to understand the pattern of organization each follows and how the maximum value of each agency can be realized.

V. The Minister of Education and the Associate Pastor

In a very real sense the minister of education is an associate pastor—an under-shepherd of the flock. All of his work contributes to the effectiveness of the pastor. For this reason many churches have given the minister of education the title of associate pastor. As church-related vocations have become more specialized, however, the title of associate pastor has been given to the staff member who assists in the pastoral ministry of the church.

1. *Various Titles Used*

Even for the person who serves as an associate pastor, a variety of titles are being used. Some churches use the title "associate to the pastor." Others refer to him as the "assistant pastor" or "assistant to the pastor." These titles indicate various degrees of relationships and supervision. There are differences in being an associate and an assistant. The term "associate pastor" carries with it the idea of more freedom, less detailed supervision, and greater comradeship in service with the pastor. These are relationships and responsibilities which must be decided by each church. The title selected for this staff member should as accurately as possible indicate his duties and relationships.

2. *Duties of the Associate Pastor*

The associate pastor is responsible to the pastor and the church. Since the associate pastor majors upon pastoral ministries, the pastor supervises his activities directly. The minister of education supervises all staff members who perform educational functions.

The duties shared by the pastor and his associate are pastoral visitation, counseling, weddings, funerals, and occasional preaching opportunities. Pastoral visitation includes calls on prospective church members, new church members, indifferent church members, the bereaved, the ill, and the unsaved.

Upon agreement with the pastor, there will be instances where the associate pastor will perform wedding ceremonies. This function will vary with the wishes of the pastor and the congregation. In large churches many ministers prefer that responsibility for weddings be shared with their associates. Other churches prefer that the pastor have this responsibility, except in cases where it is impossible for him to serve. In many cases when the pastor is absent from the city, the associate pastor conducts funerals. This service will save the pastor many special trips back to his church field from revival meetings, conventions, and other engagements.

The associate pastor will be responsible for a certain amount of pulpit supply work. In most churches he will supply the pulpit in the absence of the pastor. Other churches prefer to have pulpit guests from outside their membership. The associate pastor often conducts prayer meetings and speaks on other occasions. Sometimes an associate pastor serves as pastor of a new mission which is being established by his church. In this way the church may have careful supervision of the new work until it is self-supporting.

3. *Share in the Educational Program*

Although the associate pastor majors upon pastoral work, there are many occasions when he may share definitely in the educational program of the church. This will more nearly identify him with the total ministry of the church and will further equip him to be a successful pastor, should he feel called later to accept the full leadership of some church.

Some churches have found it desirable to call young men, immediately upon their graduation from seminary, to serve a type of internship as associate pastors, thus giving them experience in pastoral work before they are called to be pastors of churches. The major difficulty involved in such a plan is that there is a constant change of workers as these men are called to be pastors after serving a brief time as associates. Other churches have called older men to be associate pastors. Such men often major upon the pastoral ministry of the church while the pastor gives his major attention to the preaching ministry.

4

The Minister of Music—
the Minister of Education
and Music

In recent years music has become a specialized ministry in Baptist churches. The desire for an improved quality of church music, the development of graded choirs, the progress of music education, and a growing appreciation of the values of music have influenced the churches to employ full-time ministers of music.*

I. VALUES IN CHURCH MUSIC

Many values in church music have become apparent to an increasing number of church members. Music has long since proved itself as a vital ministry of the churches.

1. Serves as a Means of Enlistment

The singing of a church makes a genuine contribution to growth in membership. People are attracted to a church which has a vital singing ministry. Individuals not only enjoy listening to good music, but they also enjoy participating in congregational singing. Graded choirs which provide music opportunities for all ages attract, enlist, and keep large numbers of individuals.

---

* See also W. Hines Sims, *The Minister of Music* (Nashville: Convention Press, 1958).

2. *Cultivates the Talents of Church Members*

Music is the means by which many people express their God-given talents. A church with a graded music program begins to develop and use the musical abilities of children. The cultivation of these talents among children, youth, and adults not only helps the members to develop but also creates a spirit of gratitude and good will toward the church for providing such a program.

3. *Provides a Means of Worship*

Music is a means of worship. Individuals may worship God by singing to him their petition, praise, adoration, intercession, and dedication. Christians enter into vital worship experiences when they engage in singing the great hymns and songs of their faith. Members of the graded choirs not only participate in worship but also contribute to the worship experiences of others by singing in the regular services of the church.

4. *Creates a Spirit of Evangelism*

A singing church, as a rule, has a great spirit of evangelism. It is easy for a person to commit his life to Christ as he is influenced by the proper singing of an invitation hymn. Great revivals have been characterized not only by great preaching but also by great singing.

5. *Provides Learning Opportunities*

Music is a ministry to all phases of church life. People learn by singing. Learning takes place when people sing intelligently under trained leadership. The great concepts of theology and Bible truth are learned by singing them in choirs and as members of a congregation. The repetition of these truths by singing is another reason why music is such a valuable aid to learning.

6. *Creates Atmosphere for Christian Service*

Christians with songs in their hearts are better prepared to resume the tasks of the week after the experience of worship on Sunday. Music creates a morale which makes it possible for church members to attempt great things for God. Churches with an effective music ministry usually have a worthy percentage of their members at work.

II. The Need for a Minister of Music

In recent years an increasing number of churches have added the minister of music to the church staff. Several things have contributed to the significance of the work of this new staff member.

1. *Music a Specialized Field*

Church music is a highly specialized field. About one third of the time of the worship services is devoted to music. All church organizations and activities use music. All the people are participants. Consequently the finest leadership is desirable. Becoming a church musician requires not only years of technical training in music but also an excellent background in general churchmanship. This means that if a church is to have an adequate music program, it needs a skilled leader who is prepared not only in church music but also in such fields as the Bible, theology, history, missions, and the fundamentals of religious education.

2. *Music Programs in Schools and Colleges*

The emphasis being given to music by the public schools and institutions of higher learning have made it imperative that the churches devote more time to their music programs. Choirs, glee clubs, orchestras, bands, and other musical organizations in the public schools have given their students not only an appreciation of such activities but also the joy of teamwork. Unless the churches provide activities equally as good or better than the public schools, young people will look elsewhere for outlets for their interest in music.

3. *The Need for Vocational Leadership*

Music is a vital part of every organization in the church. Assembly programs cannot succeed without music. Those who play and direct music in the various department assemblies and group meetings of the educational organizations need training and experience to develop the skills involved. By employing a minister of music who will give attention to the development of such musicianship, a church takes a forward step toward solving its problems related to inadequate music leadership.

III. DUTIES OF THE MINISTER OF MUSIC

Although the duties of the minister of music will vary with individual churches, there are certain major responsibilities which must be accepted if a church Music Ministry is to succeed.

1. *Develop a Church Music Education Program*

A minister of music must think in terms of a total program of church music education for the church. Such a program will include more than the enlistment and training of graded choir members. Involved also is the enlistment of all church members in a program of music appreciation. This enlistment may be accomplished best by establishing a church music council which will work with the pastor, minister of music, and other church leadership in developing an adequate and comprehensive program.

2. *Train and Direct the Church Choir*

One of the most important responsibilities of the minister of music is the enlistment, training, and development of an adequate church choir. Many churches have excellent, though untrained, potential members for such a group. Other churches have fine volunteer choirs with well-trained voices. Choirs need not only training in singing but also instruction and direction for participation in the entire worship and preaching service. Choir members should co-operate fully at the time of the invitation so that the effect of the climax of the service may not be lost. A choir has a vital contribution to make to all worship services of the church, and it needs the skilled direction of a minister of music.

3. *Lead Congregational Singing*

If a church has a good choir, the members in the congregation may be tempted to listen rather than to participate in congregational singing. Often a minister of music will major upon his choirs and overlook the fact that the congregation is the largest and often the best choir he has. It is practically impossible to develop an adequate music program without leading the congregation to accept and enjoy its singing opportunities.

Congregations have definite tastes with reference to church music. A minister of music, like every educator, must begin where his congregation is and proceed to that which they do not yet fully appreciate or understand. Congregational singing is one of the truly great assets of church life. There are times when the congregation should listen, but there are other times when the entire congregation should be singing. A minister of music may make a genuine contribution to the total program of the church through developing a singing membership.

4. *Enlist and Train Music Leadership*

The minister of music should have the major responsibility for the enlistment of the music leadership of the educational organizations. He should maintain a file of prospects for these positions and work with the pastor, minister of education, age group directors, and the general and department officers of church organizations in their enlistment. As minister of music, he will, of course, take the initiative in planning a music leadership training program and maintain a program of in-service training for song leaders, organists, pianists, singers, and other music leaders.

5. *Organize and Train Special Music Groups*

It is the responsibility of the minister of music to organize and train such special music groups as the graded choirs, choruses, ensembles, trios, and quartets. As the music ministry grows, this responsibility of training must be shared with some of the more capable musicians in the church. Volunteer workers may be enlisted for the training of certain of these groups, just as volunteer workers are enlisted to teach and occupy other positions of leadership in the other educational organizations.

The graded music program begins with the Beginner music activity for children four and five years of age. The choir program proper begins with the Primary age group and should be provided also for Juniors, Intermediates, Young People, and Adults. Much attention is being given to integrating and correlating the music training program with the educational curricula and work of the church.

6. *Give Voice Lessons*

Some churches employ a minister of music with the understanding that he will give voice lessons, either private or in
classes, to members of the church who will avail themselves
of this opportunity. As individuals develop in singing ability,
the quality of the music program of the church improves.
It is understood, of course, that those who are given private
lessons in voice will sing in the choirs of the church and,
where possible, take additional responsibilities in the music
ministry. In larger churches it is impossible for the minister
of music to have this heavy responsibility if he also has to
rehearse a large number of choirs.

7. *Plan the Worship Services with the Pastor*

The minister of music has the privilege of working with
the pastor in planning the music for the Sunday worship
services, the Wednesday evening prayer service, and certain
special services. In such co-operative planning the pastor
usually gives to the minister of music, early in the week, the
subjects for his sermons on the coming Sunday. If the pastor
delivers a message at the midweek prayer service on Wednesday evening, he also indicates to the minister of music, in
advance, the topics for these discussions. In this way it is
possible for the minister of music not only to select proper
hymns but also to arrange suitable special music for these
services. If the subjects of sermons and messages can be
indicated to the minister of music far enough in advance, he
can select music and rehearse with the choir so as to have
an effective music program in keeping with the themes
chosen by the pastor. When the pastor and the minister of
music plan the worship services carefully and with prayerful
intent, the services usually proceed smoothly and effectively.

8. *Approve Special Music for Church Organizations*

The various programs of the educational organizations offer many opportunities for using those who are engaged in the Music Ministry of the church. These members should be invited frequently to use their talents by giving appropriate special music on these programs.

Sometimes members of church organizations invite musicians from outside the church to present special music for their programs. At times the special music which is given is of an inferior quality. It is a wise policy for every church to request the minister of music to work with the leaders of each organization in screening those from outside the church before they are invited to give special music. In this way embarrassing situations will not develop due to the wrong type of special music. A supply pastor would not be invited to preach until he had been carefully investigated by the proper church committee. By the same token, musicians selected should meet the standards of the church in musicianship and the choice of music to be used.

9. *Keep Equipment in Good Condition*

It is the responsibility of the minister of music to see that all pianos, organs, choir robes, hymn books, and other materials are kept in first-class condition. It is a wise policy for the church to have a contract for tuning and repairing the organ and pianos so that all instruments in the church may be tuned at least twice each year. If the instruments are moved often, more frequent tuning is needed. Choir robes should be kept in good condition so that the choir will make an excellent appearance at all services. Hymnals and music equipment and supplies should be kept in good condition and adequate supply.

10. *Present Budget Needs for Church Music Program*

It is the responsibility of the minister of music to see that the music ministry of the church is adequately cared for in the church budget. He and the music council will need to study and estimate the annual needs of the music program in advance of the preparation of the church budget. In this way he can anticipate the actual needs for the music ministry a year in advance and report them to the church budget committee for inclusion in the total budget of the church.

IV. THE MINISTER OF EDUCATION AND MUSIC

Since the beginning of the church staff program, churches have employed ministers of education and music. The person who has been responsible for education and music has been called a "combination worker." Since other combinations of responsibilities are more frequent now, one hears this title less often.

1. *Reasons for Combining These Responsibilities*

There are several reasons why the position of minister of education and music is a popular one among the churches.

There are many people who feel called of God to this type of ministry. They receive their most complete satisfactions through serving in both education and music. They not only enjoy serving in these fields but also are successful in them.

There are many churches which are only large enough to have one additional staff member besides the pastor and educational secretary. Since religious education and church music are specialized fields, a person is needed who is qualified to lead the church in both fields of work. Therefore, the churches seek to enlist and employ such a person.

The schools and departments of religious education and church music of Southern Baptist seminaries are deluged with requests for workers qualified in these two fields.

Such a demand first occurred in the 1920's when the vocations of church music and religious education were just beginning. As the churches increased in size and the programs became more complex, it was necessary for those who began as ministers of education and music to decide which of these two fields they should select as their full responsibility. Now in the larger churches many staff members who began as ministers of education and music are serving as either ministers of education or ministers of music. As this trend developed in the larger churches, another trend developed in churches of medium size. These churches have begun to develop their staff programs and are seeking ministers of education and music. Thus it seems that a chapter of denominational history is repeating itself. The demand for ministers of education and music far exceeds the supply.

By employing a minister of education and music a church may correlate these two ministries more effectively. Generally speaking, it is easier for one person to plan a correlated program involving religious education and music than it is for a minister of music and a minister of education to agree upon a comprehensive program involving their specialized tasks.

2. Difficulties with This Combination

Although there is much to be said in favor of employing a person to direct the education and music programs of a church, certain difficulties are faced when this is done.

Not many staff members have qualifications of leadership which make them effective in both religious education and music. A person of unusual abilities is needed to plan and project an adequate education program and at the same time enlist and train members in the church Music Ministry. This lack of efficiency in both fields may cause church members who are especially interested in either religious education or music to be unhappy with the leadership of a person occupying this position.

Even though staff members are interested in religious education and music, it is not often that they will take a sufficient amount of time to become properly trained in both fields. Frequently seminary graduates with degrees in church music accept positions as ministers of education and music; the same is also true of those who have degrees in religious education. In each case the position calls for specialized training in religious education and music. Without this training a minister of education and music most likely will major in the area of work he knows best and minor in the other.

The lack of skilled personnel for this combination position has led to much dissatisfaction on the part of many churches. Often a church has not known the reason for the failure of its minister of education and music. Where failure has occurred, it has not always been due to lack of preparation, but all too frequently this has been a contributing factor to lack of efficient service.

Any church desiring the services of a minister of education and music should investigate his training and experience in both fields. This is not to say that a church should not employ a person who does not have specialized training in one or both of these fields. It does mean that every church should be prepared either to help the minister of education and music strengthen himself in a particular phase of his ministry or to realize that his work will probably be less efficient in one of these fields than in the other.

As the educational ministries of the church become more highly specialized, it is increasingly difficult for one person to meet the demands which this combination vocation makes upon him. He can best measure up to the demands of his position by training a volunteer leadership to work with him. However, in maintaining graded programs of religious education and music, he will find himself in an increasingly untenable position without staff personnel to assist him in his work.

As the work of a church increases, it is almost impossible for a minister of education and music to give adequate leadership to both of these major fields. He can do so if the church provides him with a competent staff for this purpose. A competent staff would include additional secretarial help and specialized age group directors as they are needed. If such assistance is not made available to him, it will be necessary for the church to secure an additional full-time worker, requesting the minister of education and music to choose between the two fields.

The work load of a minister of education and music increased until it became apparent to him some adjustments would have to be made in his responsibilities. Essential duties were difficult to attend to. The number of workers reporting to him increased. He delegated as much responsibility to others as possible, but still his duties increased.

He discussed these matters with his pastor, who at first was not convinced that the church could afford another full-time staff member. The pastor and the minister of education and music agreed that the minister of education and music should keep a record for a week of how he spent his time, of the matters he was unable to attend to, and other pertinent information. At the end of the week they analyzed the information together. It became apparent to them and later to the personnel committee of the church that another staff member was needed.

The minister of education and music was given a choice of fields and chose religious education. The church then called a full-time minister of music.

3. *Responsibilities of the Minister of Education and Music*

In the first part of this chapter, and in chapter 3, the duties of the minister of music and the minister of education are discussed. The magnitude of the tasks of this staff member is evident when the discussions of these two positions are combined into one position. It would be practically impossible to do everything suggested in the two discussions. However, it should be kept in mind that if a church does not have a staff member to direct these activities, the securing of only one person for so many duties is a progressive step toward improving the educational and music ministries.

5

Directors of Children's, Youth, and Adult Work

When the church staff program was just beginning, ministers of education, even in the large churches, had the responsibility of directing the total educational program without the assistance of trained and experienced age-group directors.* With the development of improved materials and methods of work for all age groups, and with an increasing appreciation of the educational ministries on the part of church members, directors of children's work and directors of youth work are rapidly being added to the staffs of the larger churches.

A few churches at present are employing directors of adult work. However, in most churches the minister of education supervises the directors of children's work and youth work while he majors upon adult work himself. Enlarging the church staff by employing age-group directors provides for more careful supervision of the work which in turn results in numerical growth and corresponding efficiency in the work done.

Many factors have brought about specialization in the church educational program. These factors have varied with the major age divisions which are involved. In each instance

---

* See also Ann Bradford, *The Director of Children's Work* (Nashville: Convention Press, 1959), and Philip B. Harris, *The Director of Youth Work* (Nashville: Convention Press, 1959).

the new vocation has developed to meet a number of pressing needs.

I. NEEDS FOR A DIRECTOR OF CHILDREN'S WORK

The director of children's work supervises the volunteer workers who guide children from birth through twelve years of age. The workers who are supervised function in the Sunday school, Vacation Bible school, Training Union, Woman's Missionary Union, Brotherhood, and weekday church school programs. The supervision of the director of children's work covers the following age divisions: Cradle Roll, Nursery, Beginner, Primary, and Junior. In some churches this ministry will involve the supervision of as many as two or three hundred workers. An effective and well-trained director of children's work can share insights, materials, and methods with parents who will be able to make the home an effective force in religious education. The director of children's work also gives intensive training and supervision to volunteer workers directing the church program of training for children. There are other reasons why churches have employed directors of children's work.

1. *The Importance of a Good Beginning*

Psychology emphasizes the importance of the early years of life. The experiences of the first few months of life are highly important. Many of the basic concepts of life develop during this time. These early months also determine the quality of mental health. Since valuable learning opportunities are possible during this period, churches and parents should be convinced of the need to utilize the time for spiritual development. Making the most of every opportunity can be accomplished best through the skilled leadership of a director of children's work.

2. *Providing for Children Helps Enlist Parents*

Volunteer workers are not often interested primarily in caring for children while parents are receiving instruction and participating in worship. These workers are concerned, first of all, with providing a program of learning which meets the needs of the child. However, when such provision is made, parents desire to bring their children for these learning opportunities. Parents are often known to drive several miles twice on Sunday and at other times during the week in order for their children to have the benefit of good instruction, buildings, equipment, and skilled leadership.

3. *The Large Number of Prospects*

More than four million babies are being born in the United States each year. This high birth rate has awakened the churches to the responsibility which they face for the spiritual guidance of this vast number of children. These babies will grow up and follow some leader. All of them will have right or wrong concepts of God, the universe in which they live, the church, the Bible, themselves, and their fellow men. These concepts will be either Christian or non-Christian. Out of the vast number of unenlisted children and youth will come most of the delinquents and criminals. Churches are awakening to their responsibilities for these children and are seeking to do more to reach them.

4. *Church Nursery Schools and Kindergartens*

During World War II numbers of churches established nursery schools and weekday kindergartens to provide for the children of working mothers. After the war large numbers of mothers continued their employment and needed to have their children cared for during working hours. Other mothers secured employment and needed provision of this nature for their children. To meet this need many more churches established nurseries and kindergartens.

It seems now that the nursery schools and weekday kindergartens are in the churches permanently, and the churches are making the most of these opportunities. *The Church Kindergarten* by Polly Hargis Dillard * has been prepared for kindergarten use, and materials for use in nursery schools will soon be developed. These schools and kindergartens require the careful supervision of trained workers. There must be skilled supervision if church kindergartens are to be approved by state departments of education.

Some churches have employed full-time directors for their nursery schools and kindergartens. Other churches have employed directors of kindergarten work and have assigned to them the additional responsibilities of supervising the children's work of the church. These heavy responsibilities have made it extremely difficult for the director of children's work to serve efficiently in either capacity.

5. *The Development of Specialized Methods*

In recent years much new information has been published regarding child life and the ways in which children learn. There is a wealth of material on child psychology and behavior, as well as information regarding the methods, procedures, and techniques to be used in children's work. In fact, there is such a wealth of material that it is exceedingly difficult even for a person majoring in children's work to keep up with the progress in this area. Work with the preschool child is a major area itself. Churches are so interested in the early years of childhood that it is easy for the director of children's work to concentrate upon procedures with

* Nashville: Broadman Press, 1958.

younger children and fail to give proper attention to the equally important needs of later childhood. All periods of childhood are of equal significance and call for a large measure of specialization.

In the past it was relatively simple for a minister of education to know the entire field of religious education. Now the material is so extensive that it is impossible for a minister of education to know the entire field except in a very general way. In a large church a staff member is needed to specialize in children's work. The director of children's work who has mastered this material can effectively train volunteer workers to use these techniques effectively and so make a large contribution.

6. *Provisions Made by Agencies and Institutions*

The Sunday school, Training Union, and Church Music departments of the Sunday School Board; the Woman's Missionary Union; and the Brotherhood Commission have developed programs of children's work and materials to be used in implementing them. In addition, state departments of these organizations have vocational leaders who specialize in work with children. Schools and departments of religious education in Southern Baptist seminaries offer courses for those who plan to specialize in children's work. With such specialization taking place in the denomination, churches have felt a definite need for employing persons who can take advantage of the materials and methods which are being developed for use with children.

II. NEEDS FOR A DIRECTOR OF YOUTH WORK

The director of youth work is another comparatively new church-related vocation in Southern Baptist churches. There are many reasons why this new staff position is being accorded a place of prominence and influence in the program of the denomination.

1. *The Significance and Complexity of Adolescence*

For a long while the church education movement was primarily for children. The youth movement which preceded what is now the fully graded Training Union called to the attention of Southern Baptists the importance of the years from thirteen through twenty-four. Since the rise of the youth movement churches have become more and more conscious of the significance and complexity of the adolescent period. Unless each church provides adequately for its youth, much of the training given to children will be lost as they become adolescents. The increasing difficulty of keeping teen-agers in the churches has intensified the need for a more effective ministry to youth.

Often parents send their children to the various programs and activities of the churches. When the children become mature enough to make their own decisions and control their own conduct, they will follow the example rather than the verbal instructions of their parents. It is extremely difficult for parents to maintain the regular attendance of their children if they themselves do not attend the various services of their churches regularly.

Adolescence is a period of readjustment and reinterpretation. Many of the major decisions of life are made during this time, such as of a college or university, a vocation, a life companion, and a life philosophy. During the adolescent period young people leave home, achieve citizenship status, become financially independent, often serve in the armed forces, and make other major adjustments. It is a time of decision. Adolescents are deciding for or against Christ as Lord of life.

2. *The Need for a Positive Program*

Youth respond to a positive and dynamic program. It has been well said of youth that they are either used or lost. They are challenged by things which are great and significant. Intermediates and Young People, as a rule, do not want things done for them. They want a share in planning and conducting their own programs. If these programs are challenging and bring out the heroic, youth will respond wholeheartedly to what the church offers.

3. *The Importance of Skilled Supervision*

Working with youth requires a great amount of time, at unusual hours of the day and night. These age groups like after-game and after-church fellowships. They are happy to engage in overnight and week-long camps and retreats. They enjoy sunrise services, early morning hikes, and periods of strenuous recreation.

Activities such as these mentioned demand time and energy on the part of those who work with youth. In larger churches it is impossible for volunteer leadership to do all the necessary planning and directing of such a program. Persons skilled in the psychology and learning experiences of adolescents, in recreation, dramatics, fellowship, audiovisual aids, and related fields are needed to give complete supervision to the activities which youth requires.

4. *Enlistment of Young People in Service*

In order to keep young people identified with the work of the church, it is necessary to guide them into places of service in the church. These places of service may be positions within Young People's departments, classes, unions, and other units of organization. Larger places of service may be found in certain departments and activities of the educational organizations of the church. Someone who has the over-all perspective of church life is needed to locate positions of service and to lead young people into them as rapidly as they are prepared to assume such responsibilities.

Many young people are called of God to serve in church-related vocations. A church staff member may serve effectively in providing these young people with information regarding the opportunities which are open to them in such vocations, the duties and responsibilities of such positions, and the training required for successful service in them.

III. Needs for a Director of Adult Work

As indicated previously, only a few churches now have directors of adult work. As church memberships grow, however, this worker will come more and more into prominence. There are many reasons why a specialized worker is needed in the Adult division of a church.

1. *The Scope and Power of Adult Work*

Churches now are providing directors to supervise those who work with persons from birth through twenty-four years of age. It is reasonable to suppose that, at least in a large church, one staff member is needed to guide those who work with Adults—those twenty-five years of age and above. In this age division are approximately 40 to 50 per cent of the Sunday school's and the Training Union's total enrolment. Here are found the larger number of leadership possibilities, the financial strength, and the great majority of parents. The power of such a group is limitless; and it should be carefully enlisted and directed by a staff member skilled in working with this age group.

2. *The Expanding Adult Program*

Work with Adults is expanding rapidly. The multiple department idea has already made a great contribution to Southern Baptist growth. By multiplying departments, classes, and unions, larger numbers of Adults are enrolled and developed. Some churches now have eight or nine Adult departments. A few are planning for as many as fifteen. Many large Sunday school organizations have only a one-year range in each class of men and women for the first fifteen years of the Adult age range. Multiplying the units of Adult organization has resulted in rapid numerical growth within the Adult division. Such rapid growth alone calls for a staff member who can give his full time to this work.

3. *The Changing Psychology of Adulthood*

Modern psychology is indicating more clearly the possibilities of adult development. The psychology of the past generation held out little hope for learning and development after the age of twenty-five. "You can't teach an old dog new tricks" was the philosophy of that era. Modern psychology has exploded this myth. Adults may continue to learn throughout their lifetimes. They can learn if they desire to do so and put forth the effort.

Further, the entire period of adulthood has been studied and divided into major areas. These findings are based upon careful psychological analysis. These divisions vary in number from three to eight. This attempt to subdivide the age range of adulthood indicates the growing concept that adults are maturing people. Agreement upon the differences of adults at various stages of their maturation has led to more specific provision for adults at their various levels of development.

This information also brings with it a better understanding of the techniques which are to be employed by workers with adults. As an accurate concept of adulthood develops, some-one must keep in contact with this growing field of information and rightly relate it to work with adults in the churches.

4. *The Importance of Home-Church Relationships*

There is a growing understanding of the importance of parents in relation to the religious growth of their children. Churches are planning parent-worker meetings and programs which will enable them to work in closer co-operation with homes. Parents now are being regarded as "co-teachers" by the churches. As the value of the church-home relationship is understood, churches are becoming convinced of the need for including parents and the home in planning their educational ministries. This church-home relationship is, of course, best accomplished when there is a director of adult work who can function with the directors of children's work and youth work in such a task.

IV. DUTIES OF AGE-GROUP DIRECTORS

Although basic duties vary with the age groups, there are certain responsibilities which are common to the work of the three age-group directors.

1. *Know the Psychology of the Age Group*

It is extremely important that a director know the distinctive psychology of the group with which he works. The program of a church is a ministry to growing individuals who have distinctive characteristics at each level of maturation. No director can do his work properly unless he understands thoroughly the age level which he is to serve. Many excellent books on the psychology of child life and adolescence are available. The best of these should be carefully read and studied. Books on adult psychology are much more limited in number.

2. *Know the Organizations*

Each organization of the church came into being to meet a specific need which was not being met by other organizations at that time. Each has its own contributions to make to the spiritual training and guidance of its members.

Vocational workers should know the histories of the several church organizations, with particular insights into the factors which produced them. In this way the leaders will not only understand the organizations from the standpoint of their history and functions but will also understand more fully the objectives which may be accomplished through using them today. Histories are available in the textbooks of these organizations and in the *Encyclopedia of Southern Baptists*.

Each director should also know the significance of the Music Ministry and how it functions in the church. Although the directors may not have definite responsibility for music, they will recognize its importance in the life of every person and will seek to enlist the children and youth in the music opportunities of the church. They can assist the minister of music in the graded choir activities and work with him and with other music leaders of the various departments in relating music to the educational curriculum. They will help with choir schedules, encourage children and parents to participate in the music program, and include the music activities as a vital part of the entire program.

3. *Understand the Techniques of the Work*

Each organization has distinctive techniques for accomplishing its functions. It is necessary for the age-group director to have a working knowledge of these techniques and to understand their basic uses. Each director should have in his library the essential methods books of the organizations and their various departments. His resource materials will also include books related to all phases of his work.

4. *Co-ordinate the Work of All Organizations*

Through effective planning with key workers, the meetings and activities of all the educational organizations must be co-ordinated by each age-group director. Co-ordinating the work involves scheduling all regular and special emphases in a total calendar of activities subject to the approval of the church council and the church itself. In this manner each organization may achieve its major usefulness in the work of the church.

5. *Lead Each Organization to Function Effectively*

The age-group director must work with the pastor, the minister of education, and the volunteer workers in leading each organization to function effectively. The organization is a means to an end; the end, of course, is the contribution which the organization makes to the individual. However, the age-group director must not minimize the organizations while seeking to meet individual needs. His best work will be accomplished through the organizations, but they must be used in achieving their major purposes.

6. *Strive for Continued Increase in Membership*

One of the tasks of a church program is to lead the organizations to grow in membership year by year. In some situations where there are a large number of prospects and where adequate space is provided, this increase can be more rapid than in other situations where prospects are more limited and where space is at a premium. The age-group director is fortunate if the church with which he works can provide space as it is needed. In most cases adequate space cannot be provided as rapidly as it is demanded; therefore, the director must help the church to utilize fully all of its available space.

7. Represent the Age Group in Planning

Each director will represent his age group in planning a comprehensive church program of teaching and training. He should be a member of the church council. He should attend the meetings of the church council, at which times he will have opportunities to present the various activities connected with his work so that they may be included in the completed program. He may also report to the council on the progress of the work and offer helpful suggestions regarding better provision concerning the age group he represents. Participation in planning through this medium eliminates the necessity of having a children's council or youth council in the church.

8. Develop Christian Family Life

One of the most important duties of the age-group director is the development of Christian family life. The religious education of children and youth becomes far more effective when the active co-operation of parents is secured. Visitation in homes to interpret to parents the program of the church, the use of home curriculum materials, and frequent parent-worker meetings contribute to better understanding, fellowship, and co-operation.

There is an increasing interest in church-home relationships which is bringing about more materials, plans, and suggestions for making such relationships more effective. Leading the entire church to plan for and observe Christian Home Week each year is one of the most useful ways of magnifying Christian family life.

9. *Co-operate in Enlisting and Training Workers*

Although directors of children's work and youth work are employed to supervise the program of the church for their respective age groups, their contacts are primarily with adults. These relationships with adults center in the enlisting and training of the best possible leadership for children and youth. There are not many opportunities in a church program for age-group directors to serve in close relationship with children and youth themselves unless the director of children's work is responsible for a nursery school or kindergarten.

A director's duties are related primarily to serving with the volunteer workers. It is necessary for each director to compile a list of church members who may be enlisted to serve in leadership positions with children and youth. Such a list should be made in co-operation with the pastor, minister of education, and others who are responsible for recommending and enlisting leadership. From this list the names of prospective workers may be chosen for enlistment as needed.

It is not wise for the age-group director to have personal responsibility for the enlistment of the workers. Rather, he should place this responsibility upon the heads of the various departments and phases of work in the church and assist them in making the proper approach to prospective workers. The volunteer workers of the church will be strengthened in their positions of leadership if they have the responsibility of enlisting their colaborers. All workers who are enlisted should be recommended to the church for election. The age-group director will lead in developing an adequate training program for all who are enlisted.

10. *Co-operate in Accomplishing the Church's Objectives*

When a staff member specializes with an age division, he faces the danger of losing sight of the goal of the complete maturity of the individual. He may also fail to see clearly the total work of the church. It is easy to think of the child, the youth, or the adult as he is at a particular stage of his growth rather than in terms of the mature person he should become. It is also easy to think of the work of the church in terms of highly specialized divisions or segments. The principal responsibility of the age-group director is to join the pastor and other staff members in accomplishing the major objectives of the church. As individuals accept Christ and grow in their spiritual lives and as churches are strengthened thereby, the true objectives of the age-group worker will be accomplished.

A director of children's work accepted a position on a church staff with much enthusiasm. The prospects for happy relationships and effective service appeared bright.

She soon found, however, that the minister of education knew little if anything about children's work. When she approached him for guidance regarding decisions to be made, he pleaded that he was busy and told her to make the decisions herself. Realizing that such decisions had wide implications, she indicated that the two of them should discuss these matters with the pastor.

Fearing that she might approach the pastor individually, the minister of education consented to a conference with her, out of which came recommendations to the pastor and the church. Had the director of children's work been less understanding and tactful, a difficult situation could have developed.

Every person in a supervisory capacity must understand and appreciate the areas of his supervision and the persons he supervises. Those who serve on a church staff cannot work independently or alone.

6

Other Staff Members

Some churches have a large number of staff members who are responsible for highly specialized activities. It is not possible to discuss the duties of all staff members who are employed by such churches. The duties of several of these staff members, chosen because they are employed by a representative number of churches, will be discussed in this chapter.

I. THE EDUCATIONAL SECRETARY

The work of a secretary is important in any organization. A secretary is particularly important in the operation of the present-day church.

1. *A Significant Office*

The work of an educational secretary is so significant that this worker is often the first member to be added to the church staff. Many churches that are financially unable to employ a minister of education can afford the salary of an educational secretary. One of the first needs in every church is to set up a church office and establish a proper record system. Arranging office space and developing satisfactory procedures can be done best by someone trained in this field. In addition to secretarial responsibilities, the educational secretary can assist the volunteer leadership in their educational activities. The ministry of every pastor and church can be greatly enhanced through the service of an efficient educational secretary.

83

2. *Activities of the Educational Secretary*

The activities of an educational secretary cover almost every phase of church work. Like most church positions, this one requires a person who has the finest type of personality and abilities.

Certain responsibilities are involved in the effective functioning of this worker:

If the educational secretary is the first staff member added, she will be in charge of the church office and give assistance to the pastor in his work. If the pastor has a secretary, the educational secretary will be secretary to the minister of education and will often serve as his assistant.

One of the major responsibilities of the educational secretary is to set up and maintain adequate files in the church office. One of the most important files is an accurate roll of the church membership. It should contain such pertinent information as the name, address, and telephone number of each church member; the date he united with the church; and whether he came by baptism, letter, or statement. It is important to include the age and date of birth of each church member.

In addition, there should be an accurate roll of the membership of each organization together with an adequate financial record system. In most of the larger churches a master file has been set up, and all of the information, except financial, pertaining to each member of the church and its organizations is kept in this master file.

The purpose of an accurate roll is to provide information needed by the church's elected workers. Frequently the educational secretary is called upon to provide lists for visitation, evangelism, and enlistment.

It is extremely helpful to the pastor and minister of edu-

cation for a secretary to take care of correspondence with
members and prospective members of the church and its
organizations. The educational secretary should type letters
and maintain a file of carbon copies of all correspondence
for ready reference.

The church staff and the members of the church need a
means of communicating with each other. The educational
secretary should cultivate an attractive manner in answering
the telephone since this is one of the most important means
of public relations.

If the church issues a weekly paper and a Sunday bulletin,
the educational secretary usually has the responsibility of
typing copy for these publications. The educational secretary
must gather information of value to the church membership,
type the copy, and get the material to the printer by the
time agreed upon. If the bulletins are mailed, the educational secretary is responsible for addressing and mailing
them. If the church has an Addressograph, the secretary is
responsible for keeping the mailing list corrected and up to
date.

In many cities and towns the columns of the newspapers
are open to churches for their news. In such instances the
educational secretary often is given the responsibility of
typing copy and either mailing it to the newspaper or taking
it to the editor in person. Frequently the copy is prepared
by some other member of the staff. Where this responsibility
has been given to the educational secretary, it becomes another of her important tasks.

If the educational secretary serves with the pastor in both
secretarial and educational capacities, she may assist the
volunteer workers in their educational activities. She may
work with the general superintendent of the Sunday school,
the general director of the Training Union, and the presi-

dents of the Woman's Missionary Union and the Brotherhood in developing their educational programs.

The educational secretary must take care not to assume responsibilities which should be discharged by the volunteer workers. It is possible for the volunteer leaders of a church to overload a secretary. Many times educational secretaries do little more than mimeograph letters, cards, record forms, and other materials for the various workers in the church. The time of a secretary is valuable and should not be used to accomplish that which members of the church may do for themselves.

Of course, if a church feels this is the wisest investment of its funds, that is a different matter. However, mimeographing letters and cards for mailing can hinder the visitation program of the church, since the workers often feel that direct mail is as important as personal visitation and much less taxing.

II. OTHER SECRETARIES

As a church staff program expands, other secretaries are needed. In the medium-sized and larger churches there are several secretaries who, in many instances, may carry some of the duties which have been outlined in the foregoing discussion of the work of the educational secretary.

1. *The Pastor's Secretary*

As the work grows, a pastor will need a full-time secretary. Such a person should serve as the pastor's receptionist, answer the telephone, gather necessary information, keep a record of engagements, compile lists for pastoral visitation, and take care of his personal correspondence. This secretary may also type sermon outlines and various articles written by the pastor; she may, in some instances, transcribe recorded sermons. The pastor's secretary should check the newspapers daily for information concerning church members and call it to the pastor's attention. A complete file of materials used by other churches in publicity, revival meetings, building fund campaigns, and other special activities should be kept by the secretary for the pastor's reference.

2. *The Church Secretary*

In the larger churches a secretary is employed to keep the master file in the church office. This person is responsible for the membership rolls and keeps this information in up-to-date form. Frequently such a staff member will type various lists when they are requested.

3. *The Visitation Secretary*

In order to have an effective visitation program, some churches have employed a secretary to keep a comprehensive file and to co-ordinate visitation activities. Such churches, through their weekly visitation programs, keep in contact with their members and prospective members. Having a visitation secretary to make copies of visitation lists, to keep a file of visits made, and to provide information for effective follow-up has proved extremely successful in many churches.

4. *The Secretary to the Minister of Music*

In churches where the music program involves a large number of people, the minister of music has a part-time or full-time secretary to assist him in his work. This secretary keeps in touch with members of the graded choirs and other music organizations, takes care of the correspondence of the minister of music, maintains the music library, and assists him in various other ways. If this secretary knows music and can serve either as an accompanist or as a director of some of the graded choirs, she is even more valuable as an assistant.

III. The Church Business Administrator

In recent years a new position, that of church business administrator, has been added to the staffs of the larger churches. Prior to the addition of this position, churches employed financial secretaries who were responsible largely for keeping the financial records and otherwise looking after the business affairs of the church. As the work increased, a person with more responsibility was needed, and the office of church business administrator came into being.

1. *The Demand for This Staff Member*

There are many reasons why this new position developed in the churches:

The budgets of many of the larger churches total thousands of dollars, some hundreds of thousands. Handling such large amounts of money requires the supervision of a person who is skilled in business administration.

Receiving and disbursing money are sacred and important responsibilities which each church must accept with a true sense of stewardship. Every penny of the money received and disbursed should be accounted for to the church itself. One of the most important factors in growing a spirit of stewardship in a church is the careful accounting of all funds contributed. A person of integrity and genuine business ability is needed to supervise these matters on a full-time basis.

The present-day church finance program is highly specialized and must have trained administration. Items which are set up in the church budget must be carefully adhered to. Someone in the church who is given this responsibility can keep proper information regarding accounts before the membership. In many situations it is not possible for volunteer workers to give sufficient time to carefully supervise the complex financial programs of their churches.

2. *Responsibilities of This Staff Member*

The church business administrator has many important responsibilities which make this vocation significant. His work usually is divided into three major areas: the development of adequate financial records and the supervision of finance office personnel; the supervision of food services and kitchen personnel; and church maintenance and the supervision of maintenance personnel.

There are many types of financial record systems in use in the churches. The system best suited to the demands of the church should be adopted and installed under the leadership of the church business administrator.

The gifts of each individual who pledges to the church budget should be posted regularly in the office of the church business administrator. Many churches follow the practice of recording the gifts of all who contribute regularly, whether they make pledges or not. In the larger churches the church business administrator must have secretarial help in maintaining this record system and in other phases of his work. A record of all receipts and disbursements should be kept and included in the monthly report which the church business administrator makes to the church.

The church business administrator should prepare monthly reports which will be made to the church in its regular business session. These reports should follow an outline which has been agreed upon by the church. The church business administrator should be able to answer all questions regarding the receiving and disbursing of any church funds. Any information needed at any time by the finance committee, church treasurer, or church members should be readily available through the office of the church business administrator.

Many churches send out quarterly reports to individual contributors. Each individual thus has a record of his gifts. Where quarterly reporting of this nature is followed, the church business administrator is responsible for preparing and mailing these reports.

The church business administrator, through personal contacts, should create good relationships with business firms in his community. He should learn where he may buy to the best advantage and seek through good business practices to save as much money as possible for the church.

All debts which are made with the approval of the church should be paid promptly. Many churches have set up a system of requisitions so that any member of the church or its organizations must fill out a requisition form before making a purchase.

It should be understood that if the church budget includes certain items, it is not necessary to secure the permission of the church business administrator or church treasurer before making purchases, unless funds are not available. If money has been appropriated through the budget for the purchase of certain items, the proper requisition form should be filled out, but the fact that the item is in the budget means that permission has already been granted by the church for the expenditure.

The church business administrator should co-operate with the church auditing committee or the firm employed by the church in an annual or semiannual audit. Where church budgets are large, a semiannual audit is recommended. In smaller churches an annual audit is sufficient.

Larger churches with adequate kitchen and dining facilities have found it advantageous to have all food services and kitchen personnel under the supervision of the church business administrator. The financial transactions involved in the purchase of food, the payment for meals, and the employment of kitchen personnel are immediately related to the work of the church business administrator. Since department assembly rooms usually must serve also as dining rooms, equipment must be changed constantly and the space involved must be cleaned and maintained adequately. For these and other equally valid reasons the church business administrator usually is given the responsibility of supervising the food services of the church.

The church janitor and his assistants need someone to supervise their work. Often it seems that every member of the church seeks to be the immediate supervisor of the janitor. With one person supervising the janitor service, much more efficient work is possible. The church business administrator should also be given the responsibility of reserving various rooms in the building for use by church organizations. In this way conflicts in the use of space may be avoided, and proper janitor service may be provided for such use.

It is wise to place the church business administrator under bond. This protects not only the church but the administrator as well. Putting a person under bond is not an expensive investment, but it is one of the best ways for a church to build confidence in its financial program.

IV. The Church Hostess

The larger churches have almost continuous use of their dining rooms and fellowship halls. This requires staff personnel for supervision, service, and maintenance. These are functions of the church hostess.

1. *The Beginning of This Vocation*

As in other vocations, this particular work came into being to meet a definite need. Several factors have influenced its beginning.

Space for fellowship activities has been provided in many new church buildings. Some churches have invested large sums of money in space and equipment for dining and other fellowship activities. This investment and the use of these facilities have called for a person to supervise this phase of the work.

Church programs, to be inclusive, must provide for fellowship opportunities. This emphasis on fellowship has been extended to all age groups, with a corresponding demand for use of church facilities many times during any given week.

More and more the social life of church members is being centered once again in the churches. With houses being built on a smaller scale, there is not space within the average modern home for a meeting of very many persons. Thus groups desiring to engage in social activities must seek some meeting place outside their homes. Increasingly, church buildings must provide suitable space for such activities. As this provision is made, vocational personnel will be needed to supervise it.

2. *Duties of a Church Hostess*

The duties of a church hostess cover a wide range of responsibilities. Since many of her duties involve financial matters, the work of the church hostess usually is supervised by the business administrator. If the church does not have a business administrator, the hostess will be supervised by the minister of education or the church kitchen committee.

The social activities of the church requiring the use of the kitchen and dining room should be scheduled by some person who has this as a major responsibility.

In some churches hundreds of meals are served in the church dining room every month. Under such a heavy schedule, full-time and part-time kitchen personnel are needed. It is the duty of the church hostess to work with the business administrator and church personnel committee in employing persons who are suitable for work of this nature.

The church hostess has the responsibility for planning, preparing, and serving meals for various social and fellowship activities at the church. This type of service means that, if at all possible, the church hostess should be trained in home economics. At least she must know how to plan balanced menus and refreshments for various banquets and parties. She will need to read books and magazines which will give helpful ideas in keeping her planning up to date.

As a rule, the church will have a stated budget for the operation of its kitchen and dining room. In many churches such a budget will not include salaries, since these will be listed under salaries in the general budget. Many churches subsidize some of their fellowship activities, charging their members only a portion of the cost of regular weekly dinners. Other churches seek to make their kitchen and dining room self-sustaining by charging a sufficient amount for meals and refreshments to cover the actual costs of food preparation and serving. These churches do not attempt to recover overhead expense such as the use of the building and equipment.

Some churches have a committee to work with the church hostess in determining policies regarding the use of the dining room and kitchen and in deciding the amounts to be charged for meals and refreshments.

The church hostess is responsible for reporting, either to the business administrator or to the church treasurer, the receipts and disbursements connected with the serving of meals and refreshments each month. This report can be made a part of the total budget report each month.

V. The Church Visitor

As churches increase in size, a special worker is needed to keep in contact with church members who need special attention. The pastor and other staff members engage regularly in visitation, but because of the large number of church members, it is not possible for them to minister fully to the needs of all of those needing their services. Therefore, a staff member has been added in many churches to use the major portion of his time for contacting those who in various ways need this type of ministry.

1. *Problems of This Vocation*

Several problems are related to the work of this staff member:

The title "church visitor" is not adequate for the work of this staff member. Those who have this title often feel that they are caught on the horns of a dilemma. Some members criticize the church visitor if he does not visit them regularly. These members reason that the church visitor is paid to visit; therefore, he should visit them. There are other members who believe that if a person is paid to visit, they do not want him to visit them. They feel that since the staff member is paid to visit, his call will be professional. They prefer to be visited by someone such as the pastor, minister of education, minister of music, or other staff member because these people are not paid specifically to visit.

In order to avoid this misunderstanding, some churches have referred to these workers as church missionaries. In studying this title, however, some of the same problems

emerge as related to the former one. One of the great needs
of this vocation is an adequate title.

Further, the church visitor is not a paid extension department superintendent. A church may employ a staff member
to give his full time to extension department work. Most
churches, however, conduct their extension departments under volunteer leadership. The church visitor works with the
extension department in every way possible, but he ministers to those who can attend the regular services of the
church as well as to those who cannot attend.

2. *The Challenge of the Field*

There are many phases of the work of the church visitor
which are challenging.

Since the beginning of the staff program, the church staff
has been employed to major on securing the attendance and
participation of as many persons as possible and on improving the quality of the work for those who attend. The
staff also directs its energies toward the enlistment of church
members to participate in the fields of service within the
church.

But after continuous effort along these lines, great numbers
of church members are still not enlisted in any phase of the
church's work. Therefore, each church visitor has great numbers of church members with whom to work, many of whom
are disinterested and out-of-touch with the church.

Churches today are accomplishing their present ministry
with only a partial enlistment of their total memberships.
The loss through unenlistment is great. This loss involves
not only losses to the church but losses which occur within
the lives of church members themselves. If a greater percentage of church members could be enlisted in the full
work of their churches, individual growth would result, and

the development of church life would be vastly improved.

The function of the church visitor points up the need for an emphasis on counseling within the church. Perhaps this service could be accomplished best by an associate pastor who would major in the fields of counseling and guidance. Many people whose names are on the rolls of churches have problems which cannot be solved by regular procedures within a class, a union, or other groups. The solutions of their problems will come only through a staff member trained to discover and deal personally with these problems. Many of the persons needing special help are not now attending church services regularly. Often they promise volunteer workers they will attend, or they give various excuses rather than reasons for their nonattendance. Someone is needed on every church staff who will give personal, skilled attention to individual members who are not attending regularly and to the many regular members who have personal problems.

3. *Nature of the Work*

The church visitor has a varied and important ministry.

Many times in visitation the church visitor will find people who are prospects for church membership. After visiting with them he may distribute their names through proper channels for visitation.

If the church does not have a visitation secretary, the church visitor will work with the leadership of the church in reaching all prospective members who have been located. The visitor may serve as a resource person for those who seek information about prospective members.

The church visitor is most useful to the pastor when assisting him with various types of pastoral visitation. The pastor will plan this type of visitation with the visitor in such a way as to secure the best possible results.

Certain members of the church and its organization will need more specific attention than can be given by the volunteer workers. The church visitor has the opportunity and privilege of ministering to such people in times of special need. During serious illness, tragedy, sorrow, and other such experiences a church visitor may fill an extremely valuable place of usefulness.

Many churches have a fellowship committee which reviews cases of individual need and recommends financial assistance to such people. If such a committee exists, the church visitor will work with the members of the committee in meeting the needs of individuals.

The task of the church visitor is largely a counseling service. This worker should be trained in the best techniques of counseling and guidance. It will be helpful if he can enlist a small group of individuals who are capable and interested in counseling and train them to work with him.

VI. The Director of Church Recreation

Although the vocation of director of church recreation is just beginning, several churches now have staff members who devote their full time to recreation programs.

1. *The Rise of This Vocation*

There have been many factors contributing to the rise of this vocation.

A person develops more completely through wholesome contacts with others than in any other way. The importance of group activities is being recognized more and more. In competitive sports and in various other contacts a person's social nature is developed in an excellent manner.

With a shorter work week people have more time at their disposal today than in any other period in history. This situation has placed responsibility upon the churches for guiding the use of this time. The churches are seeking to answer this need by the employment of a skilled staff member to give direction to a well-planned recreational program.

The increase in juvenile delinquency has made church leadership conscious of the need for doing something to direct the youth of each community toward worthwhile activities. Many communities have attempted supervised youth programs. Often, in providing recreational activities for youth, they have not included the most wholesome activities. This failure to provide the best recreational program has caused churches to think seriously about making possible church-centered recreation for their own young people.

Commercial amusements are bidding for young people. Many of the operators of such amusement centers are not concerned about the moral character of their enterprises. They are concerned only with making money, even at the expense of the characters and lives of their customers. The church program of recreation has not come into being primarily to counteract such amusements, but a positive church recreational program has served this purpose.

After World War I churches became aware of the need for recreational facilities. Many of them invested large sums of money in gymnasiums and swimming pools. In providing these facilities they overlooked the need for having skilled leadership to supervise their use. Often ministers of education were asked to give some of their time to directing what was referred to as an "athletic program." Basketball, baseball, tennis, and swimming teams were organized. Volunteer leadership was enlisted and frequently did outstanding work.

Due to the lack of vocational leadership, however, many of these programs disintegrated. In cities, gymnasiums were constructed in connection with the public schools, and much of the recreational activity of the community shifted to them.

The church educational organizations expanded, and additional space was needed for them. Swimming pools in many churches were floored over, and the space converted to educational use. Gymnasiums also were remodeled to provide additional rooms for the educational organizations.

Churches are now seeking to provide space usable on Sundays but adaptable to social and recreational activities during the week. The churches which have sufficient space for educational use are constructing space especially for recreation. These are the principal churches at present which are employing directors of church recreation.

2. *Duties of the Director of Church Recreation*

The person who becomes a director of church recreation will find that he has many responsibilities.

In seeking to build a program to counteract juvenile delinquency, many church members have felt that the church recreation program was primarily for youth. Instead, however, such a program should be planned for all ages. Adults need opportunities for fellowship and relaxation as much as or more than any other age group. They carry responsibilities not only for their own lives but for the lives of those who are members of their families. The director of church recreation should plan an adequate program, graded to meet the needs of persons of all ages.

If a church has facilities for recreation, someone is needed to supervise the scheduling of the use of this space and equipment. The church with a director of church recreation usually has a recreation committee to work with him. The director and members of the committee can schedule the use of the available space to the best possible advantage.

The director of church recreation is responsible for the

wise expenditure of funds allotted to this program. He should be concerned not only about the activities of his work but about operating the recreational program within the budget allotted to it by the church.

The church recreation program should not be "another program" for a church. Rather, it should find its expression largely through the church's educational organizations. The director of church recreation should work with other members of the staff in bringing about a very close integration of recreation with the educational work of the church. When a church sponsors baseball, basketball, or football, the members of the teams belong to the church and its organizations.

The director of church recreation is responsible for providing a program varied enough to enlist as many people as possible. By varying the program he will be able to secure the participation of larger numbers of individuals.

Conducting an adequate church recreation program is a major responsibility. Such a program cannot be developed without the enlistment and training of the proper personnel. The director of church recreation should seek to enlist as many persons as possible to assist him in the development and direction of the recreation program. The ones who assist should be those who have responsibility for the social, recreational, and fellowship activities of the various groups.

In order to develop a church recreation program which will be inclusive and yet not conflict with other recreational activities, the director of church recreation should be familiar with the various recreational activities being conducted by schools, men's clubs, and other organizations in his community. If he does, the church program of recreation will not be competitive with worthwhile activities in the community but will find its rightful place in the thinking and in the time schedule of those who participate in it.

7

Leadership Qualifications
of Staff Members

The success of any staff member depends upon his ability to work with people. He must have qualifications of leadership which will make it possible for him to work with people in the democratic organization of a church. Since the success of staff members is related so directly to work with people, it is well to consider the leadership qualifications of church staff members and the ways they may cultivate a positive leadership life.

I. WHAT IS LEADERSHIP?

It is not easy to establish a working definition of leadership. Many attempts have been made to do so. Leadership has been defined as "the activity of influencing people to co-operate toward some goal which they come to find desirable." * Leadership, then, involves co-ordinating the interests, abilities, and energies of individuals into channels of activity which will enable them to accomplish their desired goals.

Good leadership has much to do with pointing out attainable goals and making such goals desirable for the group. However, a good leader will not force his opinions upon the group but will rather lead them to see for themselves

---

* Ordway Tead, *The Art of Leadership* (New York: McGraw-Hill Co., 1935), p. 20.

that certain goals are worthwhile and should be attained.

In order to have effective leadership, the group must accept the leader and the principles for which he stands. If a group does not accept the person who is in the position of leadership, they will not give him their support, and the results which he desires will not be accomplished.

This means that even though a person has a position with official status he must work for the acceptance and approval of those with whom he serves. Leadership has to be earned. It can never be conferred. Status comes from below, not from above. Each time a worker accepts a new position of service, he must work to establish his leadership with the people. His reputation for success made in another church does not guarantee his success in a new position.

II. Some Qualifications of Leadership

Every person serving on the staff of a church must have and must be cultivating certain qualifications for leadership.

1. *Called of God*

Each person serving as a leader in a church-related vocation must be called of God to his place of service. He must feel definitely that the position he occupies is God's will for his life. Like Moses, each staff member must have his "burning bush." He must have had an experience with God out of which has come his conviction that he is doing the work which God has for him to do.

2. *Love for People*

No person can serve others successfully if he does not love them. If a staff member loves the people with whom he works, he will have gone a long way toward achieving success. He must love them even when they are unlovable, difficult to understand, and critical. He will be able to love people as he sees in them possibilities for development and maturity.

3. *Physical and Nervous Energy*

Working with people makes heavy demands on energy. Dealing with problems, solving difficulties, relieving tensions, seeking to co-ordinate the interests and energies of people— all these exhaust the physical and nervous energies of the staff member. No person who is halfhearted or listless can be a leader of others. A person must believe in his task and put himself into his work to the point of expending much of his energy if he is to succeed.

4. *Sense of Purpose and Mission*

Every staff member must see in his work the purpose and mission which he has been called of God to accomplish. He must not only see in it the various details which are necessary in performing his tasks but must visualize the major objectives he is seeking. In addition to seeing clearly his part in the work of the church, he must see it in relationship to the total work of the church and of the denomination.

5. *Patience and Self-control*

Educational work is slow and tedious. Only after years of study and experience are persons considered "trained" and "experienced." It takes a long while for individuals to change habits, attitudes, and conduct. Tradition and custom are among the most difficult of all things to change. Before new procedures and methods are accepted, it will be necessary to invest much time in teaching the people the values which these new approaches represent. A staff member must be patient if results are not achieved as quickly as he desires.

6. *Willingness to Study and Work*

The position of a staff member calls for study and service. Hard work accounts for most of the success in the program of any church. Sometimes a well-trained staff member feels that the church members should recognize his training and position by responding promptly when he makes requests of them. People respond to a leader mainly because his requests are intelligent and because they like the person who makes them. A seminary degree is a great asset to successful leadership if the degree represents a grasp of the field of work. But after the degree has been conferred, a person must continue to learn if he is to become effective. When one is through studying, he is through.

A leader who will set the right example in Christian service will not have special difficulties in securing the response of the members of his church. They will be eager to follow his leading.

7. *Ability to Adjust*

The ability to make adjustments is one of the most important qualifications for staff members. Sometimes those who are reared in certain sections of the United States cannot adjust to work and conditions in other sections. Some staff workers find it difficult to change from a downtown church to a neighborhood church. Adjustments have to be made constantly if one is to be happy, useful, and successful. The necessity of adjusting continually to various situations is one of the most important things for a staff member to keep in mind. Paul wrote, "I have learned, in whatsoever state I am, therewith to be content" (Phil. 4:11).

8. *Ability to Co-operate*

Successful work in a church calls for ability to co-operate fully with others. On occasion a staff member may have convictions regarding certain matters which make it difficult for him to co-operate fully with the will of the majority. In such cases he should learn how to express his opinion without creating major problems for the church. Of course, in matters pertaining to moral life and conduct each staff member must stand by his convictions without compromise. Such circumstances rarely occur, but when they do, the staff member should always maintain a wholesome Christian attitude regarding all differences of opinion.

9. *Balanced Judgment and Tact*

To be a safe leader one must form the habit of securing full information before reaching final decisions. He must not take his daily exercise by "jumping at conclusions." Prejudice means "pre-judgment." This meaning indicates that many times opinions are formed before all of the facts are in hand. If the staff member will cultivate the practice of securing all the facts and expressing opinions tactfully, without making an issue of every situation, he will find that he can have a wholesome influence over the people he is to lead.

10. *Sense of Humor*

Every church worker should cultivate a sense of humor. The staff member should accept the truth of the proverb that "a merry heart doeth good like a medicine" (Prov. 17:22). The staff member who can laugh at himself and at situations which develop will have a much better mental attitude toward himself and his work. Many times when he is presiding over meetings where differences of opinions are pronounced and the spirit of the meeting becomes tense, he can break the tension by a touch of humor. This will prove to be the most wholesome way to handle difficult situations.

10. *Ability to Take Criticism*

Criticism comes to any person who seeks to go against the *status quo*. Sometimes church workers feel they will not be criticized if they do not take a positive stand on certain difficult issues. Nothing could be further from the truth. Workers are criticized equally for not taking a stand. By taking a positive stand which has been reached after careful evaluation of the facts involved, a worker will be better able to defend his position.

All criticism should be carefully evaluated for truth. Many times the criticisms of church members are justifiable and can serve a very useful purpose. The staff member should evaluate his life and work in terms of what he hears and seek to improve as a leader. His ability to take criticism and profit by it will cause him to be a growing leader. He should take whatever hostility comes to him—not passing it back to those who give it or passing it on to others.

11. *Strong in Faith*

Any person who is to succeed in a church-related vocation must have faith in God. He must never lose faith in God's ability to do great things. As a staff member, he will know his insufficiency, but he should be convinced always of God's sufficiency.

The staff member should also have faith in people. Even when they disappoint him, he must continue to believe that people can be changed and can become fully mature. Likewise, he must develop faith in himself. He must have a spirit neither of superiority nor of inferiority but must realize that he can do all things through Christ who strengthens him.

12. *Effective in Prayer*

It is quite true that a staff member moves forward on his knees. He must realize that he is not engaged in his work alone. God has promised his presence to those who carry out his commands. Christ told his disciples, "I am the vine, ye are the branches: He that abideth in me, and I in him, the same bringeth forth much fruit: for without me ye can do nothing" (John 15:5). Knowing these things, every staff member should seek to maintain his spiritual contacts with God through a vital prayer life. This will include not only prayer for his immediate needs and problems but also intercessory prayer for those with whom he labors and for fellow workers throughout the world.

III. Pitfalls of Leadership

The positive leadership qualifications of staff members have been considered. It is now important to turn to some of the negative elements in leadership so that the staff member may be conscious of them and the possibility of their presence in his life.

1. *Fear and Pessimism*

Fear and pessimism are among the staff member's greatest enemies. Fear of failure may lead to a sense of insecurity. This feeling militates against the worker's best interests and most efficient service. A person who is fearful will not initiate programs, since he is uncertain of their success. Often the only type of work which such a staff member will suggest is the kind to which people are accustomed. Such an attitude will rule out experimentation and the projection of programs that are advanced and daring enough to challenge the people to accomplish things which have never been attempted before. However, safeguards should be set against "wild" experimentation. A knowledge of the history of religious education will keep staff members from experimenting with that which has already been tried. A staff member must prove his ability to work along established lines before people will follow him in a trail-blazing expedition.

Some vocational workers develop a pessimistic outlook. This pessimism causes them to turn down progressive ideas suggested by members of the church. Such an attitude will chill the enthusiasm of those who may feel that the church should work toward a type and quality of work which has not been attempted before. A person in a position of leadership who is fearful and pessimistic will drive people from him rather than attract individuals to his leadership.

2. *Love of Self and Power*

Unselfishness is one of the most important qualities of leadership. Any person in a position of leadership who uses his position and authority for his own good soon disqualifies himself as a leader. Those who engage in church staff responsibilities unselfishly will have the love and appreciation of those whom they lead. This unselfishness must be more than a surface attitude. It must be a basic conviction of the staff member.

3. *Building Around One's Own Leadership*

Some individuals use their places of responsibility to advance their own interests. Some get personal satisfaction by having other people dependent upon them. They take delight in making all the decisions and in having all workers in the organization report directly to them.

This type of leader commits a grave error. The test of any person's work is how well it succeeds without him. Very few staff members will spend a lifetime in the same church. Therefore, it is vitally important that the program be built so that when the vocational worker is called to another position, his work will go on without him. Only the selfish individual will build his program around his own personality and leadership.

4. *Satisfaction over Past Attainments*

Being satisfied with previous records and accomplishments is one of the greatest pitfalls of leadership. Willingness to compete with one's own record is a great encouragement to personal growth and to the development of an aggressive church program. Each week staff members should seek to improve on the attainments of the preceding week.

In this connection the writer recalls his experiences with the first pastor with whom he served. If some new record was made on Sunday or if the results of the week's work were unusually fine, the pastor always came into the office on Monday morning with the question, "What are we going to do about next Sunday?" It seemed to the writer, who was just beginning his vocational service, that the pastor was never satisfied even for twenty-four hours. As soon as a record was made, it became history. This pastor felt that the most important decision at the beginning of a new week was to forget the past record and make another. His attitude regarding past attainments became a life principle with the beginning minister of education.

Newspapermen say that there are no yesterdays. Whatever has been printed or left out cannot be changed. A new day demands a new page. Each day the newspaper editor must start all over again. The past is dead. Can the staff member get a lesson from this?

5. *Selfish with Friends*

Each staff member must guard against the danger of having only a small circle of friends. This does not mean that the staff member will not be closer to some workers in the church than to others. However, he must have a democratic spirit and be cordial and friendly with all members of the church.

Some staff members will have problems in making friends. They find it extremely difficult to approach other people, speak to them, and in other ways express their interest in their welfare. For them, making new friends is difficult.

Qualities of friendliness can be cultivated, however. The staff member is largely dependent upon what people think of him and his work. Of course, his task is not primarily to sell himself. His task is to do the work which the church has entrusted to him. But if he will do this in a friendly way, he will sell himself without making this his objective.

6. *Critical and Talkative*

Every church staff member must guard against a critical attitude. He must refrain from criticizing individuals with whom he is displeased. Some leaders are prone to criticize freely and to be unwise in what they say in general conversation. All staff personnel should remember that nothing will harm their leadership more than to be critical of others.

Members of the church will not confide in any staff member if he is careless with the confidential information they share with him. Everything said in confidence must be kept in confidence.

7. *Unwilling to Admit Mistakes*

One of the signs of a mature person is his willingness to admit that he is wrong. Every person, in the course of time, will make mistakes. When an individual makes mistakes, he should be the first to admit them. A person's position in a church is strengthened when he admits that he has erred.

Of course, to have to admit continually that he is wrong will undermine a worker's position. To be a leader a person must be right much more often than he is wrong. Yet many people lose their leadership by blaming others and circumstances rather than accepting the blame for their own mistakes.

IV. CULTIVATING LEADERSHIP LIFE

Leaders are born in the sense that all people are born. Of course, some are born with greater capacity for leadership than others. Yet there is tremendous leadership potential in every normal individual. Each person should correctly evaluate the talents and abilities which God has given him and resolve to cultivate and utilize them to the fullest. There are many basic things which every individual may do in order to develop himself for leadership responsibilities.

1. *Give Primacy to the Spiritual*

If a person is to lead others in spiritual things, his own spiritual life must have constant attention. The church staff member, regardless of his position, represents Christ to other people. Therefore, he must give major attention to the things which will help him to build inner spiritual resources. He must be a daily student of the Bible and follow the biblical injunction to "pray without ceasing" (1 Thess. 5:17). Taking this command seriously means that the staff member must maintain the spirit of prayer throughout the day so that he may at all times be in the proper relationship with God. Whatever else he does, the staff member is to represent Christ to the limit of his ability.

2. Secure Adequate Preparation

There are effective staff members who have not had the advantage of special training for their work. However, a premium is being placed by the churches upon college- and seminary-trained personnel. The demands made upon staff members are so great that these workers need all of the formal training possible in order to succeed with their work. The type of training varies with the work the staff member does. However, for staff members who must major upon the leadership of others, a liberal arts degree and a seminary degree are considered basic requirements for the most effective leadership.

3. Learn from Experience

Although technical training is necessary, one learns most and best from experience. Upon graduation from the seminary, the worker enrols in the school of experience, from which he never graduates. In this school of experience he should be such a careful student of his work that he will not make the same mistakes over and over again. The staff member should be his own best critic, and without becoming too introspective, he should carefully evaluate himself and the quality of his work.

4. Read and Study Books and Magazines

One of the most important factors in keeping abreast of the growing developments in religious education and music is the reading program of the church staff member. He should subscribe to basic magazines in his field. He should also check book lists to discover titles of new books in his area of work. Perhaps in the future churches will provide their staff members with modest budgets for the purchase of books and magazines. From the standpoint of importance, such expenditure is more important than an allowance for car expense. A staff member with a seminary degree will soon find himself out of touch with the literature in his field unless he reads current books and magazines related to his area of work. Each staff member should pay a book bill as regularly as he pays rent on his house or payments on his car.

In arranging his program each week, each staff member should set aside a portion of his time for definite reading and study. If he does not schedule study, he will find that weeks will go by, and the pressure of responsibilities will force him to omit his study program. The mind and soul as well as the physical body must be fed. Every staff member owes it to himself and to his church to keep in touch with the best thought in his field.

5. *Follow Through with Plans*

Many steps are necessary in successfully projecting the work of the educational ministries of a church. One of these is careful planning, which many times involves a great amount of paper work. Too often staff members have made good plans, have announced them publicly, and have stopped their work at that point. Other workers seemingly have had good ideas but have seemed to be powerless in getting them accomplished. Fewer plans carefully developed and executed are better than many excellent ideas without the ability to follow through.

6. *Attend Conventions, Clinics, and Assemblies*

One of the finest ways for the staff member to keep in touch with his field is to attend various conventions, clinics, and assemblies where phases of his work are presented and discussed. Through inspirational messages, testimonies, workshop periods, and group discussions each worker may keep informed regarding the progress being made in his area of work. Attention is increasingly being given to the needs of all staff members when associational, state, and Convention-wide meetings are planned. Such planning makes possible the active participation of staff personnel in these meetings.

7. *Participate in Associational Work*

Many opportunities for personal development come through active participation in the program within the local association. Working with other churches through associational organizations widens the contacts a staff member has and gives him a broader concept of the problems and needs of the churches. In helping other churches solve their problems the staff member is in a better position to help people in his own church solve theirs.

8. *Take Refresher Courses*

During their summer sessions seminaries now are offering courses of four and eight weeks' duration which are planned especially for church staff members. Some churches have adopted a policy of permitting their staff members to take these refresher courses after a certain period of service in the churches. This is an excellent step toward keeping workers in touch with current thought in their fields.

9. *Join and Attend a Religious Education Association*

City, state, regional, and Convention-wide education and music associations are now functioning for the benefit of religious education and music personnel. Membership in these organizations is open to church staff personnel engaged in these tasks. Joining one of these associations and participating actively in its work provide one of the most significant ways for each staff member to improve his leadership life.

10. *Take Christ as Example*

The greatest obligation of every staff member is to enter into right relationship with Christ and maintain that relationship at all costs. In doing so he places himself in a position to be fruitful in the work he is doing.

The power of example is the most significant dynamic in the development of personality. Christ is the perfect example for every staff member. Not only is Christ a perfect example, but he will be the companion and guide of the staff member in all of the service which he renders. By reading the Gospels and learning how Christ dealt with individuals, how he took criticism, and how he set the perfect example, every worker should be challenged to give his best to Christ in his position of service.

One of the most helpful sections of Scripture for the staff member to read and reread is Ephesians 4:11–16. This section shows the diversity of work and responsibility in the New Testament churches and how this diversity is to be unified and properly fitted together so that it may accomplish the purpose for which it is intended. This purpose is set forth by Paul as follows: "till we all attain unto the unity of the faith, and of the knowledge of the Son of God, unto a fullgrown man, unto the measure of the stature of the fulness of Christ" (Eph. 4:13, ASV).

8

Enlisting and Developing Leadership

Since the educational ministries of a church involve work with, by, and for people, it is important that the staff member know the principles of discovering, enlisting, and training those who are to become leaders. A church must have a large number of these volunteer leaders if it is to function at maximum efficiency. The success of a staff member depends largely upon his ability not only to discover and recommend these volunteer workers but also to co-ordinate their energies into unified action for the achievement of desirable goals.

I. Discovering Leadership

In most instances those who have abilities for service in the church must be discovered by individuals who are skilful enough to recognize these abilities "in the rough." The enlistment and election of these workers should be done according to a well-thought-out plan.

1. *The People Responsible*

Most churches now elect their workers annually. In order to elect leadership which is adequate for all the organizations, many churches follow the plan of using a church nominating committee. This committee meets several weeks in advance of the date for the election of the workers and nominates the chief officer of each church organization. After their election these officers meet with the committee and nominate the department leaders. After the department workers are chosen, they in turn meet with the committee and assist in nominating the workers for their departments. Upon the completion of its work, the nominating committee submits the complete list of workers to the church for election.

Most churches do not continue the use of the nominating committee through the year. They discharge it and wait until a new slate of officers is to be elected before a new committee is constituted. In the period between annual elections it is generally understood that the pastor, the minister of education, the head of the organization, and the head of each department will constitute a committee to recommend workers for election by the church. Age-group directors of course join in the recommendations of those who are to serve under their supervision.

2. *The Necessity of Prayer*

The initial step in the discovery of workers is earnest prayer for God's guidance. There is scriptural precedent for this claim. Christ, in referring to the great number of prospects and the shortage of workers in his day, urged his disciples, "Pray ye therefore the Lord of the harvest, that he will send forth labourers into his harvest" (Matt. 9:38). As prayer is offered for divine guidance, God will be working in the hearts of those who are potential leaders and preparing them for the tasks which are to be offered to them. Since this is God's work, he will lead workers into his harvest field. Only such workers as are led by him will be permanent and well adjusted in their positions.

3. *Sources of Leadership*

There are several sources from which a list of potential leaders may be secured, the best being the church roll. As a rule, a church has a much larger number of potential workers in its membership than is generally realized. One of the major difficulties in discovering this leadership grows out of the fact that those who are responsible for enlisting workers fail to study the church roll carefully. Making a list of the positions to be filled and checking it against the church roll will reveal the untapped leadership potential in each church.

Those who work with adults can be most helpful in recommending members who have demonstrated leadership abilities in the unit organizations. Presidents of classes and unions, chairmen of circles and committees, and other officers can suggest persons who have qualities of leadership.

The unsaved and unenlisted in the community are potential workers. Winning people to Christ and enlisting them in the membership of the church increase the leadership possibilities of a church. Often church workers consider their leadership potential only in terms of the members on the church roll. It should be remembered that communities are filled with unsaved and unenlisted people who could become great leaders. Staff members should take note of the waste in human life represented by those in the community who are not Christians. This does not mean that a person should be given a responsibility in the church immediately after he becomes a Christian. However, when a person is won to Christ, he should be enlisted in the educational ministries of the church and guided in his development so that he can assume leadership responsibility in the church when he is ready for it. Too often churches have thought only of winning people to Christ without thinking of how they may lead these people to invest their lives in the full program of the church and of the kingdom.

4. *Values of a Special Committee*

Some churches which use a committee to nominate their workers annually also have a talent survey committee which serves throughout the year. This committee is given the responsibility of collecting data on all members who have leadership possibilities. The churches which have this committee also use a talent survey form for distribution among the members. The form carries with it a request for information about the previous training and experience of the members, their major interests, their hobbies, and the type of work which they would like to do in the church.

By having a talent survey committee working at the task, the church can have potential workers ready to recommend as positions become vacant or as new positions open. The information gathered by such a committee may be used by the church nominating committee in making its recommendations to the church at the annual election.

To keep the survey up to date, every new church member is asked to fill out a talent sheet the week following the Sunday he unites with the church. Through use of this talent survey, the committee can provide excellent information indicating the previous training and experience and the present interests of all church members. The value of such information is readily recognizable. The church with a talent survey committee is working constructively toward solving many of its leadership problems.

II. ENLISTING LEADERSHIP

One of the finest of all arts is that of enlisting individuals in the proper places of responsibility. This art is cultivated by careful practice and experience. How to secure potential workers is a major concern of staff members. Several fundamental principles are involved in successful enlistment.

1. *Why Members Are Not Working*

Before individuals can be enlisted, it is important to know why they are not working at some task. Many people are not at work because they feel they are not leadership material. They are so lacking in confidence that they have steadfastly refused to accept a position calling for any type of self-expression. Often this lack of confidence grows out of the high ideals which they have for those who are leaders. Those who are inexperienced have felt that if they could do their tasks as expertly as those with experience, they would happily accept leadership positions in the church. Those facing leadership responsibilities fail to see that skilled workers have spent years developing their abilities. In time, inexperienced individuals can be effective workers, also.

Lack of interest is another reason why many people are not at work. Their indifference may be explained largely on the ground that no one has ever taken time to awaken their interest in some phase of church life. The confidence expressed by the person who is seeking to enlist him will often cause the prospective worker to accept the responsibility.

Others decline to serve because they know that additional demands of time and consecration will be made upon them. Some church members seem to enjoy living on the borderline between dedicated Christian living and worldliness. They feel that more is expected of those who accept positions of leadership than of those who are only members. It is true that a worker must set the example. If his life does not measure up to high standards, his leadership will be called into question. But it is equally true that no one can

escape his obligation to live a dedicated Christian life by re-
fusing to accept a position of responsibility.

Other members of the church are not at work because
they have never understood fully what is involved in the
various tasks in a church. The writer once approached a
prospective teacher to discuss with him the responsibilities related to the office. In the course of the conversation the
prospect said, "But I can't talk for thirty minutes." This was
an opportunity to explain to him the true nature of teaching.
It was pointed out that if he could not talk for thirty minutes,
he was really more acceptable as a teacher. His inability to
lecture would cause him to share his knowledge and experience with his members through informal discussions and
questions while leading them to share their knowledge and
experience with him and with each other. This conversation
gave the prospect a new concept of teaching which led him
to accept the position.

"Because no man has hired us" (Matt. 20:7) is the major
reason why people are not at work in the churches. Most of
those who are idle have not been approached with a request
to serve. The opportunities for work have not been carefully
explained, and these people have not been correctly challenged to take up leadership tasks in the church.

2. *Creating an Atmosphere*

The pulpit ministry of a pastor is one of the most significant means of creating an atmosphere of readiness. The pastor, more than anyone else, can create a desire to serve. In
such a climate the workers will find it easy to respond.

Making public appeals for workers to take specific positions is not the proper way to enlist leadership. However,
sermons calling for people to dedicate their talents, time,
and abilities to the work of Christ will have much to do with

creating the spiritual atmosphere that is basic to the enlistment of workers. Such messages will give the proper background for the personal approach and enlistment of those
who are ready for positions of leadership.

3. *Presenting a Personal Challenge*

Only by making a visit to explain in detail the duties of
the position can one adequately deal with the personal problems involved in leading a person to accept a position of responsibility. As a rule, it is better for the one who will be
the immediate supervisor of the person to make this visit for
enlistment. For example, the department superintendent
should approach the prospective teacher for his department.
It is a mistake to employ staff members to enlist personally
the workers in the educational organizations. Their responsibility in this matter is to recommend leaders and give assistance to those who are to enlist them.

When the head of a department has sought to enlist a
worker, a follow-up visit may be needed by a member of the
church staff. If so, the proper member of the staff should
assist the head of the department in completing the enlistment of the worker. Of course, in the enlistment of the head
of an organization or the head of a department, the pastor
and minister of education should take a more active role.
An example of teamwork in enlistment is shown in the following experience. After conference with the pastor and the
general superintendent, a minister of education approached
a member of the church to serve as an Adult department
superintendent. The prospect was a person of quiet manner
but of genuine leadership ability. He was an ideal choice
for the position.

The minister of education found the man willing to listen,
but after approximately thirty minutes of monologue in

which he presented the challenge of the position, the minister of education received a flat no. The prospective superintendent gave no indication of the reasons for his answer. He could not be led into any discussion of the work. He had said no, and his answer seemed to be final.

The minister of education left the conference greatly discouraged. Upon his reporting the results of the conference to the pastor and general superintendent, the three leaders reluctantly tried to think of other prospects. They agreed to continue to pray, think about the matter further, and meet again in a few days to report any additional impressions. When they came together again, they were more convinced than ever that the original prospect was the right person.

The minister of education was asked to make a second visit and interpret the experiences and convictions of the three workers to the prospective worker in the hope that this time he would feel impressed to accept the important office.

In the second conference the minister of education engaged in a second monologue in which he gave the events following their first conference together. At the end of thirty minutes of such discussion the prospect said, "I will take it." His acceptance marked the beginning of a new day for Adult work in the church. New classes were organized which led to the addition of new departments later on.

III. Training Leadership

If an individual has been enlisted properly, he has been enlisted to prepare himself for more efficient service. One of the encouragements which may be offered to the untrained worker is that the church will give him skilled assistance in learning how to do his new work efficiently. There are many means by which a worker may be led to train himself for his task.

1. *Workers' Meetings*

Meetings of the workers, such as the weekly officers and teachers' meeting, the music council, the officers' council, and the executive committee, offer all the workers opportunities for growth and development. It is impossible to have efficient work without proper meetings. It has been said by some that churches have too many meetings. If the meetings are necessary, it is impossible to have too many of them. Perhaps this criticism stems from having too few people at work, and the same people have to attend several meetings. If this is the problem, the church should distribute its work load so that proper support may be given to necessary meetings without overworking the leaders. Every church must decide what meetings it can support adequately and plan its program in accordance with this conviction.

2. *Textbook Study*

Through training and study courses workers may secure excellent preparation for their tasks. Many churches provide several special weeks of training each year. In addition to special weeks, these same churches have study classes meeting for an hour and a half to two hours each week through the year. Such classes often meet one day a week—in the morning, afternoon, or evening—to provide training for those who can come at these particular periods. Before the schedule is made, the workers are consulted as to the time of meeting which is most convenient for them. Because of thoughtful planning there is hearty co-operation in such a study program.

For those who cannot attend regular study classes, training and study course textbooks may be completed through home study. Under this plan individuals read the books and answer all questions listed in each book. Many individuals have completed their diplomas in this manner.

3. *Use of Records of Training Work*

One of the most helpful means for encouraging the development of workers is the use of adequate records on training work. A complete record of all awards should be kept in the church office as a ready reference for those who are seriously pursuing their training program. Being able to give personal guidance in the choice of books which should be studied is an important factor in training the workers. If a person is working to complete his diploma courses, his study will have direction and purpose. Awards should be requested promptly. Often the awards are kept in the church office and presented in a special service. Some churches recognize the training achievements of their workers through commencement exercises, banquets, or other means.

4. *Conventions, Assemblies, and Associational Meetings*

The training opportunities of conventions, assemblies, and associational organizations is exceedingly valuable. Hearing testimonies about successful churches, coming in contact with enthusiastic workers, and discovering how other churches are solving their problems are among the most helpful experiences individual workers may have in such meetings. Those who have contacts with members of other churches have a wider concept of their work and participate more enthusiastically in the activities of their own churches.

5. *Observation*

Churches which are looking ahead in the solution of their leadership needs have found that one of the best means of getting potential workers ready for their work is to offer them training through observation. Before a worker accepts the full responsibility of his task, he visits experienced workers and observes them at work. Sometimes this observation takes place in the worker's own church. Sometimes the worker in one church will visit another church to get ideas on how to do his new tasks acceptably.

6. *Practice*

Practice teaching and practice leadership are excellent means of preparing a new worker for his task. Sometimes an individual is elected to serve as an associate worker instead of being given full responsibility for an office at once. Serving as an associate enables him to gain experience before he is elected to full leadership later. Such a practice builds confidence and enables the worker to begin his task far more efficiently than if he did not have the practice.

7. *Directed Reading*

If a church has a library or if books may be borrowed from a personal library, it is well for the staff member to recommend the reading of certain books as one phase of the training program. There are excellent books which do not appear in the training course or study course listings. It is helpful for the workers to read such books. Often it is not necessary to read an entire book but only certain chapters which have special significance for the tasks involved.

8. *Personal Conferences*

One of the best ways to train workers is through individual conferences. Many problems emerge in personal conversation which would never come to light in group meetings. In this way problems may be solved, and the leadership of the worker is strengthened. The staff member who can budget his time so as to provide for such conferences will be more effective in his work.

9. *Audio-Visual Aids*

Excellent films and filmstrips are available for training workers in the churches. Most areas of leadership training are covered by these materials. In the field of administration, filmstrips are available on the duties of officers, the necessary meetings and councils, grading, records, committee work, and other significant activities. Filmstrips on teaching and training may also be purchased and used to improve the quality of the work.

Additional materials are being produced constantly. Staff members will find that the use of audio-visual materials will enlarge the learning opportunities of the volunteer workers and accelerate their experiences of learning.

IV. KEEPING LEADERSHIP

While staff members should give major attention to enlisting leadership, they need also to see the importance of keeping leadership. The rapid turnover of workers in church organizations is a major problem. In some large churches there are numerous vacancies in the organizations soon after the new church year begins. In many instances these vacancies are indicative of faulty enlistment methods, lack of clearly defined objectives, and the absence of encouragement.

1. *Problems of a Changing Leadership*

It is impossible to have permanence and stability in the educational organizations where volunteer workers are changing constantly. Some churches seem to feel that since the election of officers is on an annual basis, the heads of the organizations should be changed each year. In other churches these officers serve only one or two years. The purpose of the annual election is to improve the quality of leadership in the church. Electing workers annually makes it possible to tone up the leadership of the organizations. In no way should the annual election be interpreted to mean that the leadership must be changed annually. The workers who are giving satisfactory service should be re-elected year after year. Those who are not serving properly should be given an opportunity to improve or be replaced. Every church needs to study its own problems in this area and do everything possible to stabilize its leadership.

2. *Making Leadership Permanent*

There are many ways in which the tenure of church leadership may be stabilized. These and other methods should be used to give continuity to the service of the workers.

At the time of enlistment the responsibilities, duties, and privileges of the proposed office should be presented to the prospective worker. Such matters as planning, preparation, visitation, attendance at regular planning meetings, training opportunities, and any additional responsibilities should be explained fully. The prospect should not be told that he will have little to do, that the church will require nothing more than the barely necessary. Christ demands the best of his workmen. His work and its requirements should be explained fully when the worker is being enlisted.

Appreciation should be expressed when effective work is done. It is amazing to find that in many churches workers have rendered faithful service for years with little or no expression of appreciation for what they have done. Staff members should be conscious of the fact that volunteer service is a labor of love and should watch for every opportunity to express gratitude and appreciation to those whose work is effective.

Every staff member is busy, but he must never be too busy to have time for the people who need him. If he is unapproachable and unresponsive, he will have to replace workers constantly. Of course, he must be careful not to encourage workers to seek his counsel when they should be seeking the counsel of their immediate supervisors. However, there are times when he and he alone can give the help which the worker needs. He must provide time for such conferences as the workers find them necessary.

No staff member should ever be guilty of recommending a little program to a church. God is great, and his program covers the entire world. He is worthy of great programs and great planning on the part of those who serve him. He has committed a world task into the hands of his followers. This task involves reaching every person in the world with the gospel of Christ.

Any plan within a church that does not seek to take the gospel to every person is inadequate. The world purpose of Christ should be kept before every church. The church's work in relationship to that program should be carefully set forth. Christ's objective means not only that the churches shall seek to win every person, but also that they shall provide for the spiritual growth and development of every person who is won.

Keeping these great objectives before all the workers will help them to see themselves in relationship to the world mission of Christ. If these great purposes can be made clear, they will keep the workers serving devotedly at their tasks.

The service a person renders is significant, but sometimes this fact is not clearly understood by the workers. They need to realize how important their work is. They are dealing with growing lives. Some of their members may be as weak and vacillating as Simon Peter. But when these members are brought into the proper relationship with Christ, they can become rocklike in character. Each one who works with growing personalities can rely for assistance upon the truth of the inspired Word of God, the leadership of the Holy Spirit, the transforming power of Christ, and the grace and love of God. Surely no task on earth is as significant as the one which involves the souls of persons. The staff member should lead every worker to see his opportunities in the light of this truth.

IV. METHODS OF LEADING PEOPLE

Every staff member should master the methods of working with people. There are many excellent books dealing with principles of leadership. Only a few methods of leading people will be discussed in this chapter.

1. *Take Personal Interest*

One of the finest ways to lead people is to let them know that they are valued highly as individuals. The expression of personal interest will develop normally if a person has a basic love for people. It is easy for a staff member to lose interest in people who are not working actively in positions of leadership. If a worker resigns, the staff member should still feel a personal interest in him. Otherwise the leadership of the staff member will be injured seriously. Having a genuine regard for personality, cultivating a friendly and cordial attitude, entering into experiences with people, and showing interest and concern identify the staff member with those whom he seeks to lead. There is no substitute for personal concern.

2. *Get and Give Suggestions*

People follow their leaders better when they feel free to make suggestions regarding the improvement of their work. Each staff member should encourage this freedom of expression. Being willing to listen does not mean that every suggestion made will be accepted but that the staff member will be anxious to know all points of view. One of the necessary elements in leadership is willingness to listen to the opinions of others. If the art of listening is cultivated, it will not be long until every staff member will be getting information which will be of genuine value to him in the planning and directing of his work.

3. *Treat People Differently*

There is a measure in which every person must be treated in the same manner. To express this thought another way is to say that every staff member must be democratic. There is another sense, however, in which workers must not be treated in the same manner. Each person is a different personality and must be treated differently. Some workers enjoy levity; some are serious. Some are very sensitive; some seem to be insensitive to criticism or to lack of attention. These qualities must be known by the staff member, and every person under his leadership should be dealt with as his personality requires. Such personal attention requires time and study, but this principle is essential in leading people effectively.

It is interesting to study the various personality traits represented by the twelve disciples. Jesus dealt with these men on the basis of their individual differences as well as their common characteristics. Being able to select as followers such different personalities and blend them into a united group is but another indication of Jesus' masterful leadership.

4. *Make Experiences Pleasant*

One of the aims of staff leadership should be to bring out the pleasure involved in service. Too often service is looked upon as drab and colorless. Work with people is one of the most exciting of all activities. Since behavior is unpredictable, meetings with groups of individuals can be one of the most thrilling and challenging of all experiences. The joy and happiness resulting from Christian service should be known by every worker. If a person is happy in what he is doing, he will receive lasting satisfactions from his service.

Each staff member should strive to make clear to all the workers the opportunities which Christian service makes possible for them. He should not be pressing them so hard for results that he and they will miss the most significant values of their work.

9

Solving Difficult Problems

Members of church staffs face many problems, some of which are particularly perplexing and difficult to solve. It is the purpose of this chapter to consider certain common problems and possible solutions to them.

I. Finding a Place of Service

Staff members have constantly wrestled with the problem of how to find their places of service. Some have felt that they should do nothing other than wait for the Lord to lead them to a field of work. Others have sought places of service. Currently there is such a heavy demand for workers that this problem is not as acute as it was when the vocation was just beginning. Graduates of seminaries often are confronted, several months before their graduation, with a number of opportunities for service.

But after a worker has spent some time in a position, he may feel that his work has been accomplished. It is then that he feels led to seek another field, and he wonders what is the best procedure for doing so. There is no substitute for finding and following the will of God with reference to a place of service. If a staff member has a continuing impression that his work with his church is finished, this could be an indication that God has other work for him to do. Other factors may cause staff members to feel that they should make a change in their work. Of course such a change will not be taken lightly; the staff member will be sure of the need for a change.

1. *Do Not Apply*

A place on the staff of a church is different from a position in the business world. In the latter case a person is free to apply for a position which he knows to be vacant. In churches this practice is frowned upon. It is felt that the office should seek the man, not the man the office.

2. *Inform Personal Friends*

God uses human agents in his divine plan. If a staff member will let his friends know that he feels he should change his work, this information may be used to bring the vocational worker and his new field of work together. Churches appreciate such recommendations, and those who make them are helping both the churches and their fellow workers.

3. *Contact Denominational Leaders*

When a person desires to be in touch with another place of service, it is well to notify denominational leaders. In the case of seminary graduates, their professors can be of invaluable service in making recommendations. State secretaries of Sunday school, Training Union, Brotherhood, Woman's Missionary Union, and Church Music are sometimes helpful in making recommendations to churches. Denominational servants employed by Southern Baptist Convention boards and agencies may also prove valuable in giving assistance to vocational workers desiring contact with churches. Professors and other denominational workers are not obligated to recommend a worker for a church position. However, most of them are glad to be of service in this matter.

4. *"Take It to the Lord in Prayer"*

Although it is helpful to let his friends and denominational leaders know of his desire to change his work, the staff member must not rely too much on them. He must not assume that they will find him a place to work. He has been called of God into a definite field of service. He has dedicated his life to this service and must seek, above everything else, to know the will of God concerning the work he is to do. Only by prayer and by following the leadership of the Holy Spirit may he be fully satisfied with the decision he makes with reference to his place of service.

When a staff member is dissatisfied and unhappy, he should make his dissatisfaction a matter of prayer. Often after earnest prayer he can adjust to the circumstances of his position and serve more faithfully where he is. At all times he needs to face his problems squarely and seek to master them in the power and grace of God.

II. FINDING GOD'S WILL

When a staff member has been approached by a church and has the opportunity of accepting or rejecting the new place of service, it may be quite difficult for him to find the Lord's will. Several things will prove helpful to the staff member during his time of indecision.

1. *Opportunities for Service*

Every staff member should be certain that the position open to him offers opportunities for service. He must make sure he does not confuse these opportunities with material advantages. The church with the largest membership does not always offer the staff member maximum opportunities for service. As a rule, it is better to help build a situation than to inherit one which is well on its way to achievement. The joy of Christian service is found in joining with a group of dedicated church members in the task of growing a great church. Whatever else a staff member may be looking for, he should be convinced that his position offers him the opportunity to serve others to the limit of his ability.

2. *The Challenge and the Appeal*

The challenge and the appeal which the new situation offers should be helpful in reaching a decision. The vocational worker should ask himself such questions as these: Does this place offer opportunities for the full expression of my desire to serve? Are there large numbers of people to be reached? What are the possibilities for expansion and development? Does this position appeal to me? Is there a great future in this new work? These are questions which, if answered, will give guidance to the staff member in making his decision.

3. *A Sense of Desire and Happiness*

It is doubtful whether the Lord will lead a person into a position that does not offer the promise of happiness. The work may appear difficult, but the consideration of it should create a desire to accept its difficulties and achieve success in spite of them. Most of the world's great leaders have found happiness in difficult situations. If a staff member can feel a great attraction toward his work, this feeling will be another means of assurance for him.

4. *The Attitude of the Committee*

A staff member can learn much about the new position from his discussions with the church committee. Some committees are interested primarily in securing a worker to lead them in achieving numerical results. Others are interested in increasing the budget or the prestige of the church. Most committees will be interested in securing someone who will help them in developing a ministry to growing Christians. As the staff member talks with the members of the committee, he can usually ascertain the emphases of the committee and of the church. The attitudes revealed in such discussion are indicative of what he may expect in the new position and should be carefully considered before a decision is reached.

5. *The Response of the Church*

If the worker visits a church and talks with its members, he can tell by their response whether a few rather aggressive members of the church are seeking to expand the staff or whether the entire church is committed to the program which he is to lead. His impressions may not be accurate unless he talks with those who represent a cross section of church opinion. Members often are hesitant to express themselves readily, so the staff member will need to be a keen student of human nature if he is to secure the information he needs.

6. *Conviction After Prayer and Dedication*

Using all of the human factors which have been discussed is quite helpful in reaching a decision. However, the only way to fully determine the Lord's leadership in the matter is to reach a decision after prayer and the full commitment of one's life to Christ.

Since each person has only one chance at life, he does not want to make a mistake in the way he invests his life. He will need to know very clearly what God's will is for him and be willing to put his desire to do God's will above every other desire. If he does these things, any person considering a staff position will be able to enter into the most difficult situation knowingly and convincingly. He will feel that the difficulties involved are a challenge and that God has chosen him to do these difficult tasks because of his willingness to find and do his Master's will.

III. "What Should I Do First?"

After a staff member has accepted his place of service and has arrived on the field, his major problem is what to do first. Often he is expected to work a transformation overnight. Whatever he does should be based upon accurate information. Several major areas of church life should be diagnosed carefully.

1. *Study the Attitudes of Church Members*

Attitudes and ideals regarding a church program vary with churches. Some church members have had an excellent background of training and experience and are ready for an aggressive program. Other church members are undeveloped in these areas, and time is required to determine what their attitudes are.

During the time the worker is getting acquainted and studying his church field, he should be analyzing the various attitudes of the members of the church. He should seek the answers to such questions as these:

Do the members have a spirit of willingness and co-operation?

Is there a desire for the entire church program to advance?

Are members interested only in the portion of the program where their major interest lies?

Are workers with adults eager to co-operate in discovering potential leadership in their units of organization?

Is the church evangelistic?

Is there a spirit of Christian fellowship among the members?

Are church members ready to work, or have they employed the staff to do their work for them?

As the staff member finds the answers to these questions, his program will be taking direction. He should discuss these matters with the pastor, and together they should seek to evaluate their information. They should not discuss their analysis with any members of the church except the most trusted leaders who can also help with the evaluation.

2. *Survey the Building and Equipment*

Since the educational program is determined by the amount and type of space which is available, the staff member should study the church building carefully. He should first determine if all available space is being used. Sometimes, by adjusting the meeting places of various age groups, additional space may be gained. At times additional units of organization may be placed in the church auditorium and balcony, the kitchen, the parlor, the choir room, the robing rooms, the furnace room, and various other places. The staff member should go over the entire building and determine whether the best possible use is being made of the available space.

He should also decide whether provision has been made for all age groups. He should make a checklist of such questions as:

Is the space for the children's departments adequate?

Are there sufficient classrooms for Intermediates and Young People?

Has the church provided space for married Young People and young Adults?

Are there movable partitions between alternate classrooms of the Junior and Intermediate departments?

Are there as many classrooms for men as for women?

Is there an adequate room for choir rehearsals?

Is there storage space for music and choir robes?

Should additional property be purchased?

Are there residences, apartment houses, or store buildings within the same block as the church building? If not, is there additional property nearby?

Can parking space be acquired and used to an advantage?

Is better equipment needed? Equipment is a vital part of any building program, although many building committees do not realize this fact. Too often churches have spent all of their money erecting buildings and have not given sufficient thought to the equipment which is needed.

Well-chosen equipment is vital to the successful work of the educational organizations. Too often more furniture is bought for the children's departments than is actually needed. Quite frequently old tables and chairs are donated by the members. If this is the best the church can do, such furniture can be used. However, many churches would provide much better equipment if they realized its importance. It is impossible to do the best work without good equipment. Perhaps one of the most important steps in the improvement of the work will be the purchase of new equipment.

Is a building program needed? It may be a long while before the church can actually have a new building, but if a building is needed, the staff member should play a major role in leading the church to recognize this fact. Should the church appoint a survey committee and develop a master plan? The building is the tool with which the staff is to work. The improvement of space and equipment is a major responsibility of every staff member.

These questions involve the future growth and development of the church and should be included in the diagnosis made in the early days of the staff member's service.

3. *Evaluate the Present Organization*

The present organization of the church should be carefully evaluated. Does the church have an efficient Sunday school, Training Union, Brotherhood, Woman's Missionary Union, and church Music Ministry? If the church has provided these areas of ministry, the worker should raise these questions regarding them:

Do they provide for all age groups?

Is each organization growing satisfactorily?

Do the enrolments indicate that each age group is being reached properly?

Is the organization balanced as to leadership?

Is the best leadership concentrated in one organization, or is it equitably distributed among all organizations?

Does the church give the proper emphasis to each organization?

Is each one given its proper amount of time in the church calendar?

Is there need for enlarging all or some of the organizations of the church?

Such a study of the needs of a church will cause a thoughtful staff member to plan a program in keeping with needs which must be met if the church is to move forward in its work.

4. *Begin When Reasonably Sure of Success*

The staff member who begins his work by attempting many things and succeeding in few of them will soon lose whatever leadership promise he may have had. It is extremely important for him to be reasonably sure of success before he attempts to lead any phase of the church program. Unless certain general needs are pressing, it may be well for him to begin work in some limited area or with some particular organization where there is already a recognized need for his assistance. If the new staff member can prove his leadership in a situation of this kind, this success will assist him in gaining acceptance in larger fields.

A minister of education being interviewed by a pastor and committee regarding the leadership of the educational program of their church was much impressed by the description they gave of their plans for the future.

At their invitation he visited the church. The church property was located in the heart of the city, surrounded by buildings which made expansion out of the question. The church, however, was united in plans for enlargement. At that time the purchase of a five-acre tract near the downtown area was contemplated, but plans regarding the purchase of the property still were incomplete.

Impressed by the spirit and optimism of the members, the minister of education accepted the call of the church. Later the new property was purchased and plans were developed for a complete building program, including auditorium and educational space. When construction on the buildings began, the minister of education launched an intensive program for discovering, enlisting, and training leadership for the anticipated enlarged organization. He enlisted all adult class members in a week's study of adult organization, grading, and promotion under leadership from outside his church.

When the new building was completed, the leadership for the new organization was trained and ready. The adults reorganized themselves without major difficulty. The church accomplished the greatest work in its history, soon was debt free, and is now planning additional educational space.

In all of his planning the minister of education stayed in constant contact with his pastor and the volunteer workers in the church. He invested his knowledge and resources in planning the building, securing adequate equipment, and preparing the entire church for the fullest utilization of their investment.

IV. Establishing and Maintaining Right Interpersonal Relationships

The staff member's relationships with others is of great significance. He must cultivate personal qualities which make him not only acceptable but desirable to his fellow workers. Each staff member must give consideration to various groups with whom he has close personal association.

1. *Interpersonal Relationships with Church Members*

Since every staff member serves the members of the church, it is extremely important for him to understand them. The proper understanding between the worker and the members is established in various ways.

The staff member will work to gain the friendship and confidence of the church members. While the worker is making his adjustments with the members of the church, they are also adjusting to him. The staff member must prove himself to be a leader before members of his church will be willing to follow him. He should be affable and friendly without being superficial. He must attempt to see the entire work of the church without bias or prejudice.

He should attempt to learn the names of as many of the members as possible. He should learn where they live and the work in which they are engaged. Leadership does not develop overnight. It comes after months and even years of the staff member's proving himself to be trustworthy, thoughtful, and dependable.

He will also study the church situation. Churches have common problems. The difficulty of the problems will vary with each church. If the staff member is to succeed, he must be a student of the particular problems and needs of his own church. Procedures which work well in one location may not work equally well in another. Each worker must draw upon all of his training and experience in seeking to meet the needs of his situation.

Every program must be adapted to the special needs of the church. A program which has worked successfully in one church may not be used with equal success in another. The principles will not vary, but the ways in which these principles are applied vary somewhat in every situation. If plans and programs grow naturally, they will have a much greater opportunity to succeed.

Leaders with abundant energy are prone to maintain their work at high pressure. Some workers are perfectionists, more concerned about having the work done perfectly than in developing the people who are doing the work.

A certain amount of activity must be maintained if a volunteer organization is to be kept intact. It is also true that a great amount of work must be done if the organization is to achieve anything like its basic purposes. However, it should be realized that the development of Christian character is not achieved through undue pressure from a highly organized program. The staff member should lead his members in their own spiritual growth and create within them a desire to reach all unreached people of the community for similar growth.

There is no substitute for visiting individuals in their homes. In a large church it will not be possible for staff members to visit in the homes of all the members regularly. However, those in leadership positions should be visited soon after the staff member arrives on the field. Leadership is established more quickly and firmly when the staff member knows each of the workers.

Some staff members have felt that they do not have time for such contacts, especially at the beginning of their ministry. The fact is that they must take time for something as important as personal visitation. Visitation should have priority in a time schedule in any given week. It is a most important investment of time in the beginning of one's work and throughout one's ministry. Of course, the worker's visitation activities should be planned in staff conferences.

Attending meetings of departments, classes, unions, circles, and committees affords the staff member the opportunity of becoming personally acquainted with members of the educational organizations. Through these contacts he may also become acquainted with people who have leadership possibilities. He will not be able to continue attending all such meetings after his program has become established. The workers will understand the necessity for limiting the number of meetings as the demands upon his time become greater. If, however, in the beginning days of his work he will accept invitations to meetings, he will find such contacts extremely beneficial.

A minister of music who had spent most of his life in states west of the Mississippi was called to a church in a southeastern state. He was totally unfamiliar with his new state, city, and church. Soon after his arrival he went to the public library and selected several books on the history of the state. From the Chamber of Commerce he secured printed materials on the history, growth, and development of his city.

When these materials were read, he began reading the minutes of his church. In a few weeks he was one of the best informed citizens of his community. When he spoke, he referred to events of historical interest in his state and city. He knew of important events in his church which were known or remembered by only a few of its members. He rarely referred to his home state or the churches he had served. This was not done for effect but that he might identify himself as soon as he could with the members of his congregation.

This was typical of the way in which he approached all of his responsibilities during his tenure of service. He soon knew the level of music appreciation of the church, but instead of forcing certain types of music on the members, he tactfully introduced them to the best forms of music. Needless to say, his service with the church was happy and successful.

2. *Interpersonal Relationships with Church Leadership*

The term "church leadership" is used in this discussion to indicate those who hold positions in the church by election. This includes such groups as deacons, Sunday school officers and teachers, Training Union workers, officers of the Woman's Missionary Union and the Brotherhood, people elected to the Church Music Ministry, members of church committees, and other church officers. All of these individuals are important in the life of a church. As quickly as possible, every staff member should establish a working relationship with them.

Upon entering a new situation there is a temptation to "clean house." To attempt radical changes in the leadership or the program is usually detrimental to success. Of course, if major changes must be made and if an agreement has been reached in advance regarding them, such prompt changes will be in order. In such cases it is usually better to make major changes at once rather than to delay them for several months. However, to make "a clean sweep" at once simply to suit one's preconceived ideas is a grave error.

As far as possible, each elected officer should be permitted to continue in his traditional place of responsibility. Many workers have been in the same positions over long periods of time. Some may be inefficient and unsuccessful. However, before they are changed to other positions, a serious attempt should be made to challenge and inspire them to do more with their responsibilities. Certainly major changes are not in order until the staff member knows the church situation and the abilities of the volunteer workers.

The church-elected leaders should be consulted before plans and policies are determined. If the church does not have regular planning meetings for the workers, establishing these meetings is perhaps the most important initial step to be taken by the staff member. These meetings are important because they offer the church staff and the volunteer leadership opportunities for consultation. If it is not possible to have regular planning meetings at first, there should be special meetings in which plans and policies pertaining to the development of the total church life may be discussed.

It is important to approach such meetings without too

many preconceived ideas. The staff member should have
carefully thought through his plans and should conduct his
conferences in such a way that the volunteer workers will
feel free to express themselves. The wisdom and judgment
of those who have been loyal and faithful to the work of the
church through the years are needed in the development
and projection of an adequate program.

Serious mistakes are often made during the first few
months of the staff member's tenure of service. Such mistakes make it difficult for him to succeed. If he will think
through his plans carefully and urge the church leadership
to attempt reasonable goals, he will gain their good will
and esteem. It is much better to proceed gradually, on firm
foundations, than it is to make rapid progress for a time and
then to experience a marked reaction.

3. *Interpersonal Relationships with the Pastor and Other Staff Members*

Harmonious relationships within the staff are imperative.
The ability to work with others in close personal relationships is one of the indispensable qualifications of a staff member. Churches have been severely handicapped and even divided because of wrong relationships among staff members.
It is a serious matter for any worker to draw his salary and
at the same time hinder the work of his church.

The pastor and other members of the church staff must
face the fact that they will know more about one another
than others will know about them. Such close personal contacts may mean increased admiration or keen disappoint-
ment. It is possible that staff members will present one facet
of their personalities to church members and another facet
to one another. Staff relationships call for the finest type of
Christian personalities.

There must be a careful matching of personalities if a staff program is to succeed. Individual differences make it almost impossible for certain people to work together. Yet if an attempt is made to understand each other and if reasonable allowances are made for individual differences, there can be harmonious relationships.

All staff members face serious difficulties in working for a while with personalities of certain types and then, after changing their field of work, finding themselves serving with others who are totally different. The ability to adjust to various types of situations and personalities is necessary if one is to be a successful staff member.

In their adjustments with the pastor, staff members are responsible for many factors in developing wholesome relationships. Often staff members are overly zealous for professional recognition. They should remember that they have entered a comparatively new vocation which is slowly gaining recognition. Recognition will come as the work of the staff member succeeds.

Sometimes staff members make the mistake of planning and projecting a program which is independent of the other work of the church. Much confusion will be avoided if the entire program is planned under the supervision of the pastor. The minister of education should not refer to the educational work as "my" work. The minister of music should not refer to music as "my" program. Although each worker should be identified with his work in such a way that it is "his," he does not possess it. The minister of education and the minister of music direct the education and music programs as trusts of the church. These programs will be continued by the church should the present staff members take up work in other fields.

Vocational workers should not run ahead of pastoral leadership. If a pastor does not fully appreciate what the staff members are seeking to do, time to show him the advantages of such work is required. Often staff members seek to build leadership about themselves. The leadership they exert comes in conflict with the leadership of the pastor.

The program of a church is one program with the pastor as the leader. By sharing his ministry with one or more staff members, the pastor can serve all members of the church. This shared leadership is one of the major causes of difficulties in interpersonal relationships within the staff. In matters of religious education and music, the pastor should recognize the leadership of staff members. As one pastor well expressed it, "I am the leader of the total church program, but in his field each staff member is my leader." If the workers plan their work together, they will have a unified program. If not, there will be serious conflict.

For a time one of the pastors' major objections to programs of religious education and music was that these programs seemed to be displacing the traditional services of the church. This objection is being rapidly overcome where the programs center in the life of the church. A pastor is the spiritual leader of the entire church. This means that the pastor gives leadership to the staff and to the education and music programs as well as to the general life of the church.

Some pastors expect their staff members to take care of numerous details, most of which are relatively unimportant. It is a mistake to employ real leaders and overburden them with details which could be cared for by members of the church on a volunteer basis.

In the larger churches there are several staff members with specialized responsibilities. One might think that there would be few, if any, problems of interpersonal relationships in a church with a number of workers. Yet many problems develop unless someone is responsible for supervising the staff personnel.

By virtue of his position the pastor has this supervisory responsibility, but most pastors organize their staffs so that this responsibility is shared with other staff members. Unless there is understanding regarding these matters, the possibilities of misunderstanding and friction mount. Several suggestions may be offered for improving relationships within the staff.

All staff members should respect the pastor's leadership. They may differ with his decisions at times, but they should respect his right to make them. Decisions by the pastor which do not favor one certain program should not be taken personally. The staff member can help to create a wholesome attitude toward the pastor by the manner in which he follows his leadership.

Jesus taught that the highest positions are attained by rendering the greatest service. Workers on the staff should not be concerned primarily with the prestige of their positions but with the service they render. In the plan of God every position is important. A minister of education could not do his work effectively without an efficient secretary. She will rarely be mentioned when his work is recognized, and yet she shares vitally in his success. He should remember this and seek to create the finest possible working conditions for his secretary. This interest in others should be included in all relationships of all staff members with all those with whom they work.

One of the benefits of working as a staff member is that the total work load can be adjusted so that each member may have a day each week for rest and relaxation. The fact that the work can be shared within the group and that there can be close personal fellowship should encourage every vocational worker to devote himself to the development of the right spirit within the staff.

4. *Maintaining Good Interpersonal Relationships*

Staff members should be the best friends in a church. If they seek to harmonize their differences on all issues, very little misunderstanding will exist. This does not mean that staff members will always be in complete agreement. They should, however, confer and pray together so that their principal differences may be reconciled.

When one staff member is criticized, this criticism should be the concern of all. A staff program is hindered by one inefficient worker. Every member of the staff should seek not only to fill his place adequately but to give encouragement and assistance to the other members in their work. No staff member should encourage criticism of another.

The all-inclusive program of the church should be planned with all staff members participating. Time should be given each week to staff meetings. Planning the work together helps to prevent misunderstanding and strife.

Staff workers should engage in periods of fellowship and recreation together. Some churches encourage their staffs to spend a few days together each year and use this time for planning their work. In order to concentrate upon their planning, some staffs have gone to nearby places where they could work without interruption. Such planning has given direction to staff work and has improved the morale of the members.

Each member of the staff should realize that he is, first of all, a Christian; he should seek to be Christian in all that he does. It is inevitable that misunderstandings will arise and tensions will develop among staff members. When these situations occur, those who are involved should face these difficulties in a true Christian spirit. With self-control and forbearance there should be a frank discussion of the problems involved, and a solution should be reached. If the workers fail to reach a solution among themselves, they should talk with the pastor about their differences. In prayer and in the right spirit these tensions can be resolved without creating difficulties within the church.

By all means, conflicts between staff members should never be aired among the church members. Knowledge of such conflicts will cause factions to develop, and the fellowship of the church will be injured. The church is far more important than any staff member. Every worker should be willing to pay whatever price is necessary in order to maintain the fellowship of the church.

V. Status for Church Staff Members

Within recent years there has been a growing feeling that ministers of education and ministers of music should be given definite status by their denomination.

The first official action taken by the Southern Baptist Convention on this matter was largely a declaration that the status of education and music workers was a matter for each church to decide. The Convention so expressed itself at San Antonio, Texas, in 1942 by adopting a resolution brought by a special committee. The report of the committee was as follows:

The question of the status of Religious Workers other than regularly ordained or licensed ministers of Baptist churches having been brought to the attention of the Southern Baptist Convention and referred to this special committee, we recommend the adoption of the following statement:

In our opinion we, as a Convention, have no authority to determine for any governmental agency the official religious status of a Baptist. This authority is vested solely in the congregation of a local Baptist church.*

On January 7, 1947, the Inter-Seminary Conference of the Southern Baptist Convention adopted the following resolution:

Whereas, hundreds of young men have felt called to give their lives to full-time religious service in the fields of Religious Education and Sacred Music, and

Whereas, they do not have official standing in the eyes of the denomination, the civil authorities, and other agencies, thereby suffering handicaps in status and in privileges according to other full-time religious workers,

Therefore, the Inter-Seminary Conference of the Southern, Southwestern and New Orleans Baptist Theological Seminaries in session at Seminary Hill, at Fort Worth, Texas, January 7, 1947, does hereby petition the Southern Baptist Convention to pass the following statement:

"This Convention hereby recognizes Religious Education and Sacred Music as religious vocations, suggests that the churches officially certify those men who give evidence of a divine call and purpose to give full time to these vocations, recommends that they be given such consideration as this status merits, and requests that the names of those so certified be printed in its annual directory." †

Dr. J. M. Price presented this resolution to the Southern Baptist Convention in St. Louis in 1947. After discussion by W. R. White and John D. Freeman, it was adopted.

After this action by the Convention, churches followed various policies in giving status to vocational workers in the fields of religious education and church music. Some churches licensed the workers. Others ordained them to the

---

* *Annual of the Southern Baptist Convention,* 1942, p. 90.

† *Annual of the Southern Baptist Convention,* 1947, p. 40.

ministries of religious education and music. In such ordination the regular procedure for ordaining pastors has been followed. The major difference has been that instead of ordaining these workers to the gospel ministry, they have been ordained to the work of religious education and church music.

Some churches have ordained ministers of education to the gospel ministry. These churches interpret the ministry of New Testament times to be broad enough to include the work of religious education.

These three major practices present a confused picture so far as the denomination is concerned. Yet since the churches are autonomous, no Convention resolution regarding procedure can be binding upon them. As churches have experience in this matter, doubtless a pattern will emerge in keeping with Baptist tradition which will care for this problem.

Feeling the need for a more comprehensive study of the entire problem, the Southern Baptist Convention, at its session in Kansas City, May 30, 1956, authorized the appointment of a special committee on church-related vocations. The committee was directed to study the demand for workers in church-related positions, particularly in the fields of missions, religious education, and church music. It was instructed to seek proper means of confronting young people with the opportunities and possibilities of such service.

The committee was also requested to suggest provisions for appropriate recognition and status for those serving in church-related vocations. It was asked to recommend a unified and effective procedure for encouraging the enrolment of such young people in Baptist colleges and seminaries to the end that they might be adequately equipped for their divinely appointed life work.

This committee was appointed immediately. Dr. Allen W. Graves, dean of the School of Religious Education, Southern Baptist Theological Seminary, Louisville, Kentucky, was named chairman. Seventeen committee members, representative of many phases of Convention interests, were named to serve with him.

This committee reported its findings to the Executive Committee of the Southern Baptist Convention in December, 1956. The adoption of its report created a new position, church-related vocations counselor, at the Sunday School Board and authorized the development of a complete file of all volunteers for church-related vocations. The adoption of the committee's report also called for the publication of adequate guidance materials for volunteers, parents, and pastors.

John M. Tubbs, state Training Union secretary of Virginia, was elected church-related vocations counselor by the Sunday School Board and began his work on April 1, 1957. The committee was continued for another year to work with Mr. Tubbs in initiating the new program and to give further consideration to the problem of status for those entering the fields of religious education and church music.

In its final report to the Southern Baptist Convention in Houston, May 23, 1958, the committee presented this statement, which was adopted, regarding the status of nonpastoral workers:

The committee believes that recognition grows out of service rendered. Status should be based on the scriptural function performed. The committee believes that the ministries of Bible teaching, Christian training, and church music are scriptural functions of the churches needing divinely called leadership, and that God is calling individuals to serve in these positions. We believe that the Holy Spirit is leading the churches to seek the more than 3,000 workers needed in these church-related vocations and that these positions should be filled with God-called people who are adequately trained.

We believe furthermore that the churches may recognize the divine call of such individuals through the call of a church to such positions and through installation, certification, licensure, or ordination as the Holy Spirit may direct the local church.

Concerning the growing practice of ordaining men serving in nonpastoral ministries it is recommended that no men should receive such ordination until the church membership is convinced by the Holy Spirit that such individuals have been called of God to such ministries. Such individuals should possess and demonstrate to a church and to an examining council, the high qualifications for ordination set forth in the New Testament.*

With determined effort on the part of the denomination to give assistance to those who are called of God to church-related vocations, it becomes increasingly important for the position of the denomination regarding the status of church staff workers to be clarified.

---

* *Annual of the Southern Baptist Convention,* 1958, p. 426.

10

Planning and Promoting
the Work

The success of a staff member is determined not only by the amount of leadership ability he has but also by his skill in planning and promoting an adequate program of work. He should keep in mind that he is primarily an educator. He must have a thorough understanding of the content of the educational program. He should know curriculum materials, principles of learning, and the scriptural significance of individual growth and development. He must understand how these things may be shared with the largest number of people.

These are the things he is to promote and advance. He is not to become an activist promoting a series of events and emphases simply because he feels the workers should be busy. The staff member must not promote promotion; he is to promote education.

A story is told of a man who was shingling his roof in a fog. He worked so rapidly that he shingled out into the fog and fell off the roof. Promotional programs often run ahead of educational programs in the same manner, and often little is accomplished.

I. PLANNING A PROGRAM OF WORK

There are many values in planning effectively. The staff member can prove these in his own experience.

1. *Time Budgeted Wisely*

One of the privileges of serving on a church staff is that the staff member has the opportunity of budgeting his own time. However, the freedom involved in determining a schedule can result in catastrophe. Since the staff member is free to plan, he may waste time and prove himself incapable of using the hours at his disposal to the best advantage. Individuals who cannot organize their own activities will find it impossible to organize for others efficiently.

2. *Worthless Ideas Eliminated*

By careful planning ideas which have little value are eliminated. No "half-baked" ideas should be presented to a group of workers for discussion and adoption. A church member, commenting on the numerous suggestions of a staff member, said, "He has hundreds of ideas, and some of them are good." Careful planning will help staff personnel to suggest only plans which are of the greatest significance.

3. *Spur-of-the-Moment Decisions Avoided*

A successful businessman whose major problem was his moodiness told how he had learned to work with his moods. His system called for planning when he was feeling at his best. But rather than projecting these plans immediately, he waited until he was in a pessimistic mood and revised the plans made previously. In this way he balanced his planning between moods of optimism and pessimism with much success. When individuals act hastily and plan beyond their means of accomplishment, major problems result.

4. *The Entire Staff Included*

Since the program which is planned affects the entire church, plans which are developed should be discussed with the staff before being referred to the church council and the church for adoption. The opinions of several workers will tend to give balance to the suggested activities. Questions which are raised will force a careful evaluation of all the factors involved. In discussing plans with other staff members, the problem of communicating plans to them is solved also.

II. Planning a Program of Personal Study

Not only is the planning of a church program important, but the planning of the staff member's own study program is especially significant. The staff member's field of work is constantly developing. New materials are being produced, and new procedures are being developed. Unless the worker is striving diligently to keep abreast of current thinking, he will soon find himself out of touch with many new developments in his area of responsibility. Therefore, a comprehensive study program must be planned and maintained.

1. *Develop Worthy Study Habits*

Since every day will call for participation in many activities, a staff member will be tempted to take part in those which are most pressing and will fail to make suitable preparation for his major tasks.

Every staff member should have a regular time for study. If at all possible, a portion of every day should be spent in this way. If he relies upon daily study, his study time may cover only short periods. Very few staff members will have enough time to read a book at one sitting or study for a prolonged period. Extended study can be done only as he can arrange to be protected from the usual telephone calls and flow of requests for his services. Since time for study is at a premium, portions of time each day must be devoted to it. If a staff member expects the busy workers in his church to be prepared, he cannot claim that he does not have time to study.

If at all possible, each vocational worker should have a special place for study. This place does not have to be a room with a personal library, although such surroundings for study are highly desirable. A table where books are accessible will be a helpful place for study and preparation. The room in which he works should be well lighted and ventilated. Included in the study habits of the minister of music should be regular practice time in his performing medium and advancement in all areas of musicianship.

2. *Build a Personal Library*

Every staff member should have a growing personal library. One is tempted to invest his money in everything but books and magazines. Some years ago a survey was made of pastors' libraries. Every pastor who was serving in a lengthy pastorate had a large and well-balanced library. A library is an investment in one's leadership life and future.

3. *File Helpful Materials*

Such materials as magazine and newspaper articles, booklets, and pamphlets should be carefully filed for reference. There are many excellent filing systems. One which seems to meet the worker's needs should be adopted. Materials in the files should be kept up-to-date for ready reference.

4. *Balance the Study Program*

Although each worker must read and study in the field of his major interests, he should broaden the scope of his study so as to include related fields. Certainly the Bible should be read and studied regularly. In addition to using the suggested lesson course materials, the staff member should engage in his own plan of Bible study. This may be a study of the Bible by books, topics, or biographies or according to some other plan.

Books on psychology and counseling should be bought and read. Books which deal with personal enrichment and leadership should be included in one's reading and study program. Helpful sources regarding the newest books are publisher's book lists and book reviews in professional journals.

III. ARRANGING A WEEKLY SCHEDULE

It is quite difficult to plan and keep an adequate weekly schedule. This difficulty develops because it is impossible to schedule everything which will come into the scope of work in any given day or week. However, without some attempt at planning, much valuable time will be lost daily and weekly.

1. *The Importance of a Schedule*

Needless to say, unless the staff member has carefully thought through a regular work week and attempted to budget his time every day, he will not be able to take care of the necessary functions of his office. Certain days of the week call for certain activities. The schedule on Sunday follows the same basic outline throughout the year. On this day the worship services are conducted, the Sunday school and Training Union meet, and the Music Ministry functions in its fullest expression. Most of the visible results of the week's work will be accomplished on Sunday. These results may be anticipated because of such activities as visitation for enlistment and evangelism conducted during the week. The organizational planning meetings held on weekdays are largely in preparation for the results which are anticipated in the services on Sunday.

The Brotherhood, Woman's Missionary Union, and graded choirs must meet between Sundays. Such meetings advance the training of church members and lend support to the total work of the church. In addition to these meetings, other groups will meet regularly for recreation and fellowship. In a well-organized church all of these meetings fall into a regular schedule. In this framework of meetings and activities the staff member must plan his personal program.

The basic activities of each day should be scheduled in broad outline. Enlistment of new workers, planning and developing the program, personal study, personal efforts for enlistment and evangelism, preparation for various meetings, publicity, and promotion of the work must be included in careful planning within the period of every week. In addition, time should be planned and kept for recreation and relaxation.

2. *Difficulties in Staying on Schedule*

Because a church program is subject to the problems and needs of people, it is impossible for a worker to stay on a rigid schedule. Interruptions will come from many sources. Illness, death, and various personal needs and problems of the members may call for visits and conferences which were not scheduled at the beginning of a week.

These and related matters often cause staff members to give up all semblance of a regular schedule. In the light of these problems, trying to stay rigidly on a schedule will cause frustration. The worker who makes a schedule can also make adjustments to it and should do so as circumstances require.

However, confronted with the problems involved in staying on schedule, most workers agree that they get far more accomplished by having a schedule than by not having one.

IV. Promoting an Adequate Program of Work

Many outlets are open to church staff members for the promotion of their work.

1. *The Church Council* *

The most important meeting for planning and correlating the total church program is the church council. This organization is composed of the pastor, church staff members engaged in the education and music programs, the chairman of the deacons, the Sunday school superintendent, the Training Union director, the Woman's Missionary Union president, and the Brotherhood president. Members of church committees are invited to attend the meetings when their counsel is needed. As a rule, the pastor serves as chairman of the council, but in many instances this responsibility is delegated to the minister of education.

The council may meet subject to call by the pastor. However, most functioning church councils meet monthly to plan the program of work, evaluate what is being done, and set up the planned program in a calendar of activities. The calendar usually is printed and distributed among the members after its adoption prior to the beginning of the church year.

2. *Weekly Cabinet Meetings*

Some ministers of education have found it desirable to have weekly cabinet meetings of the Sunday school and

---

* J. M. Crowe, *The Church Council* (Nashville: Convention Press, 1957).

Training Union. Each cabinet is composed of the general officers and the heads of the departments.

There are several values in having these meetings. They have a unifying effect. Weekly meetings give an opportunity for discussing mutual problems and planning the work. The workers develop a sustaining fellowship which encourages them in their tasks. Through cabinet meetings the vocational and volunteer workers may share ideas, and the activities of the organizations may be more completely centered in the total life of the church.

If such meetings are held, it will be impossible to have them simultaneously. Church staff members are involved in work with both groups and find it impossible to divide their time between meetings which are in progress at the same time. Also, the duplication of volunteer leadership in Sunday school and Training Union makes it necessary for some individuals to make a choice between two simultaneous meetings.

Some churches having weekly Sunday school and Training Union cabinet meetings have found that luncheon meetings are valuable. This plan is usually most successful in downtown churches where the leaders are within easy reach of the church. Neighborhood churches find it practically impossible to have such meetings at noon.

Often the Sunday school department superintendents meet for thirty minutes prior to the weekly officers and teachers' meeting on Wednesday evening. This is an excellent procedure for the Sunday school, but it leaves the Training Union at a distinct disadvantage since this organization has only a monthly planning meeting, as a rule. If cabinet meetings can be held only in the evenings, the Sunday school cabinet may meet on Wednesday evening prior to the officers and teachers' meeting, and the Training Union cabinet may meet before the Training Union on Sunday evening.

The programs for these meetings should be kept simple and informal. The agenda should include reports from the previous Sunday, a review of the activities scheduled in the church calendar, the presentation of new plans, the discussion of any new policies and programs, and at times prepared discussions dealing with special problems and needs and remarks by the pastor and other staff members.

3. *Staff Meetings*

The importance of a weekly meeting of the church staff has already been referred to. Doubtless, if more churches had such meetings, the general tone of church staff life would be vastly improved.

At least once a week the staff should have a meeting of sufficient duration to review its work and project its program. It would be helpful if the staff could meet twice each week. Some church staffs meet on Monday to plan their work for the week and on Saturday to evaluate what has been done and to pray and plan for the services on Sunday.

Other staffs meet each morning for a brief period of prayer, meditation, and discussion of the day's work. Where daily meetings are held, highly efficient work is observed. Under the policy of daily meetings it is not necessary to have lengthy sessions.

The time of meeting will depend upon when the staff members can get together. As a rule, one member of the staff is asked to answer the telephone during staff meetings. Some churches publicize the time of staff meetings and request church members not to call the church office at that time.

The program for a staff meeting varies with the church. The following outline is suggestive of what may be done in a weekly meeting of the staff.

It is well to begin the meeting with a period of devotion. There are numerous ways to vary this period. It may be led by staff members who serve in rotation. Some staffs have the custom of memorizing a verse of Scripture, which serves as a key verse for the week. In the staff meetings these verses are given from memory. A Scripture passage in keeping with the major emphasis of the church may be selected and read.

After the Scripture is read there should be a season of prayer. In this period certain departments and their workers may be remembered by the staff members. Frequently staff members pray for these same departments and workers throughout the week. Prayer may be offered for those who will be making special efforts in evangelism and enlistment. If workers are needed, there should be special prayer for them. In addition, the sick, the bereaved, the unsaved, and the unenlisted should be remembered. Staff members certainly should pray for each other and the effectiveness of their ministries.

After this period of devotion various matters will claim the attention of the staff. There should be an evaluation of the various records for the week, such as attendance, additions, visits, and offerings. There should be reports on progress in soul-winning, mission activity, and enlistment. Advance in the several phases of the church program should be reported on by the staff members, with special attention to problems and needs. The responsibilities for the coming week should be considered, and attention should be given to sharing these responsibilities among the members of the staff.

Every effort should be made to establish perfect freedom in these meetings so that the communication of ideas will be effective and the finest interpersonal relationships may be established and maintained.

A church experienced difficulty in keeping its staff. No

member remained longer than two years. There were no serious problems in the church, salaries were adequate, and there was a wholesome attitude toward staff members. What, then, was the difficulty in maintaining an adequate staff?

When the situation was analyzed, it was found that the staff as such never met. The members rarely saw each other. Although there was some attempt at supervision, actually none existed. There was no communication of plans within the group. There were no group objectives, no division of responsibility, no teamwork. Members of the staff wondered why they never accomplished much, although they worked hard. The church members wondered why some members received a great amount of attention while other members were overlooked.

Although there were significant things to be accomplished, the staff never met to plan and pray for their achievement. When the need for regular meetings of the staff became apparent, they were established immediately and rigidly adhered to. The morale of the staff was lifted, and a noticeable improvement in the work of each member was detected immediately.

4. *Organizational Meetings*

The planning meetings of the church organizations give excellent opportunities for promoting and projecting the educational program. In instances where the staff members work through volunteer Sunday school superintendents and Training Union directors, they will assist these workers in planning the programs for these meetings. The basic planning meetings in a church program are the Sunday school weekly officers and teachers' meeting, the Training Union executive committee meeting and officers' council, the church music council, the Brotherhood executive committee meeting, and the executive committee meeting of Woman's Missionary Union. Discussions on planning and conducting these meetings may be found in the regular textbooks of these organizations.

Needless to say, these meetings will not succeed without careful planning and preparation. Many times they are attempted on a regular schedule without first insuring the training of the workers and their commitment to make the meetings succeed. Simply announcing meetings does not guarantee attendance or success. Each meeting must be planned so carefully that the workers will receive helpful guidance for their tasks. The staff members should devote time each week to planning for these meetings.

5. *Enlargement Campaigns*

One of the most effective means of planning and projecting programs of Sunday school and Training Union work is the enlargement campaign. This is a period of intensive work for one week in which a survey is made of the possibilities for membership in an organization, classes are conducted each night in the study of methods and procedures related to the work, and visitation is carried out each day to enlist workers and enlarge the organization.

The most frequent use of the enlargement campaign is during the week prior to the time a church enters its new educational building. In many cases such campaigns are directed by skilled leaders from outside the church membership who are enlisted for the purpose of aiding the church in making an objective study of its work and in enlarging its organization.

The date for such a campaign must be set well in advance

in order to secure the skilled leadership necessary to conduct it. Workers for such a campaign involve a campaign director and a worker for each age division. In making such provision for leadership, the church makes an investment in its present and future programs.

When an enlargement campaign is conducted under successful leadership, the results may be measured in terms of numerical growth, the winning of large numbers of individuals to Christ, and the development of the entire church in missions, stewardship, and evangelism.

V. PLANNING FOR DENOMINATIONAL RECRUITMENT

The staff program has long since passed from the stage of experimentation to a position of absolute necessity among the churches.

Southern Baptists have been growing churches faster than they have produced vocational leadership to meet their needs. Hundreds of trained workers are needed to fill church staff positions which now are open or which will be open in the near future. The great demand for these staff members indicates the appreciation and esteem of the denomination for the important positions which these staff members occupy.

As the work of the churches expands, a corresponding expansion of associational, state, and Convention-wide organizations to serve these churches is also taking place. Skilled workers in religious education and church music are needed in all these areas.

One of the great privileges of the staff worker is to interpret the demands for vocational leadership, the positions which are open, and the type of preparation needed to those who feel called of God to church-related vocations. By assisting them to respond to their call and prepare themselves for service, the staff member makes a great investment not only in them but also in the future of his denomination. Above all else, he must be certain that he sets before these volunteers an example which will attract them to these significant areas of Christian service.

Code of Ethics
for Church Staff Members

My Call

God has called me to serve him in the field of church-related vocations. Because my life is dedicated to him, I have responded to this call.

It is my conviction that God has called me to my position on the staff of my church. I accept this position as a place of trust and an opportunity for service.

My Aims

I shall use every opportunity to win the unsaved to saving faith in Jesus Christ. I shall attempt to influence those with whom I work to do the same.

Believing in the doctrine of Christian growth, I shall encourage every Christian to "grow up into him in all things."

Instead of building a program which centers in myself, I shall direct my energies toward strengthening the total work of my church.

Since I am concerned about the growth and development of my denomination, I shall make every effort to participate in denominational meetings and work.

My Preparation

Realizing my need for spiritual power, I shall strive to read my Bible daily and to "pray without ceasing."

Since physical energy is so important to my work, I shall follow a schedule which will help me to be physically ready for my responsibilities.

I shall be diligent in reading and studying so that I may develop and maintain sufficient resources to give adequate leadership to those with whom I work.

My Conduct

I have resolved to seek "first the kingdom of God and his righteousness."

I shall be a true steward of all of life's resources and shall strive to lead others to practice the same principle.

I shall strive to live a life above question and reproach.

I shall deal honestly in all of my business relationships, living within my means and paying all financial obligations promptly.

My Interpersonal Relationships

I shall co-operate fully with my pastor, recognizing his leadership of the entire church program.

I shall co-operate with fellow staff members in planning and developing a correlated program of work.

It is my desire to understand the total work of my church and relate myself effectively to it.

I recognize my responsibility to the members of my church and shall give first consideration to them and their needs in carrying out my tasks.

As a citizen of the world I shall remember my obligations to the world mission task. It shall be my purpose to help provide more churches and missions for the unreached and to share more fully in missions around the world.